Classics

NORTHAMPTONSHIRE
COUNTY CRICKET CLUB

Mal Loye, who in 1998 became Northamptonshire's first triple-centurion for forty years.

Classics

NORTHAMPTONSHIRE
COUNTY CRICKET CLUB

ANDREW RADD

TEMPUS

First published 2002
Copyright © Andrew Radd, 2002

Tempus Publishing Limited
The Mill, Brimscombe Port,
Stroud, Gloucestershire, GL5 2QG

ISBN 0 7524 2431 9

Typesetting and origination by
Tempus Publishing Limited
Printed in Great Britain by
Midway Colour Print, Wiltshire

Anil Kumble.

FOREWORD

BY DAVID CAPEL (NORTHAMPTONSHIRE AND ENGLAND)

What makes a Northamptonshire classic match? Easy. We win the toss on a sunny morning, bat first on a belting pitch and set off at a nice, steady eight runs an over, courtesy of Geoff Cook and Wayne Larkins. 'Ned' completes a typically flamboyant hundred – ensuring that yours truly doesn't have to get the pads on too early and can enjoy a decent lunch – before flicking one off his legs down to deep mid-wicket, where the fielder holds a brilliant catch on the boundary.

Peter Willey comes in at number three and bashes it around for a bit, paving the way for Allan Lamb to dominate proceedings with a 70-ball century – the fastest of the season. We declare at 350 for two, and then let loose Curtly Ambrose and Greg Thomas, who try to outdo each other with the new ball. Kevin Curran nips a few out in the middle and Northamptonshire, leading by 200 or so, decide to bat again. An opportunity, perhaps, for the rest of us to make a few. We eventually set a target and manage to dismiss the opposition on the stroke of time, Ambrose knocking out the last man's middle stump with a superb yorker.

Ideally, that victory would be over Leicestershire, our oldest local rivals, or Warwickshire. We had some wonderful tussles with the Bears during my career – probably inevitable when you look at the quality of the cricketers on show. When high-class performers and real personalities like Allan Donald and Allan Lamb lock horns – or Dermot Reeve and Anil Kumble – the rest of the players in the two teams will tend to raise their game and you are likely to see something special. A game that you'll remember in colour rather than black-and-white.

Our match against Warwickshire at Edgbaston in 1995 was one of several exceptional contests we were involved in that summer. It was a fantastic feeling to play in such a confident side, with every member of it believing that anything was possible. Even when we found ourselves in the direst of situations – seeing Nottinghamshire pile up 353 for one on the first day at Northampton, or being bowled out for 46 by Essex at Wardown Park – everyone was prepared to back himself, and back the man next to him, to turn things around.

As a spectator with the rest of my family, I was lucky enough to see Northamptonshire win the Gillette Cup at Lord's in 1976. I also saw Allan Lamb's runs help us to the Benson & Hedges Cup four years later. Those sort of occasions in a club's history should never be forgotten. Andrew Radd cares passionately about Northamptonshire cricket, both its past and its future, and hopefully this book will help to keep alive memories of some great days for our county.

David Capel.

ACKNOWLEDGEMENTS

My grateful thanks go to a number of individuals who have assisted one way or another in the preparation of this book. Firstly to David Capel for writing the foreword; if he can instil in his young Academy charges just a little of the fierce pride in playing for Northamptonshire that was one of his own trademarks, then the future should be bright at Wantage Road.

John Watson's magnificent collection of Northamptonshire photographs has provided many of the illustrations, and others come courtesy of Northamptonshire CCC, Pete Norton, Mick Cheney, Tony Kingston and the *Northamptonshire Evening Telegraph*, who have also allowed me valuable access to their extensive newspaper library in Kettering. As ever, the staff at the Central Library in Northampton have been most helpful, patiently dealing with my many requests for material on microfilm.

My thanks also go to Dennis Brookes, Ian Davies, Stephen Coverdale, Graham Alsop, David Steele, Alan Hodgson, Mal Loye, Ian Davidson and Jim Lyon for their help and interest; likewise to James Howarth, Rosie Knowles and everyone at Tempus Publishing.

INTRODUCTION

The record books show that Northamptonshire have won just under a quarter of their first-class matches since achieving promotion from the ranks of the Minor Counties in 1905. In my personal selection of 50 games, from Fred Spofforth's canter on Northampton Racecourse to Mike Hussey's record-breaking performance 120 years later, the success rate is eighty-two per cent. This choice, therefore, clearly does *not* constitute what the opinion pollsters would deem a 'representative sample.'

Just another one-eyed, scarf-wearing fan? Well, possibly. But the first definition of 'classic' in my dictionary is 'of acknowledged excellence.' Does defeat by an innings and 484 runs at the hands of Warwick Armstrong's 1921 Australians fit that particular bill? What about the 1987 and 1990 NatWest Trophy final disasters against Nottinghamshire and Lancashire? Or being hustled out for 12 by Gloucestershire in 1907? Northamptonshire's long-suffering supporters can be described as many things, but never as a bunch of feckless pleasure-seekers; a spot of cheerful distraction from the all-pervading gloom of the West Stand will do them a power of good. In other words, let's enjoy ourselves for once.

My first visit to Northampton's County Ground was on 29 May 1972, a few days short of my tenth birthday. Barry Richards and Richard Gilliat made some runs for Hampshire against an attack led by John Dye and Ray Bailey, and David Steele responded to my teatime request for an autograph with 'Not now, son.' Later that season, I sat with Uncle Dudley – a cricket-loving musician who, as a boy, watched J.T. Tyldesley bat for Lancashire – in the 'cut-off' seats at the football end, and witnessed the County's seven-wicket victory over Ian Chappell's Australians. An unforgettable occasion and probably my own 'number one' in this half-century of memorable encounters, just ahead of the 1976 Gillette Cup final and Mal Loye's triple-century against Glamorgan.

Hunter S. Thompson, rarely seen at Wantage Road – although 'Fear and Loathing' is a not unfamiliar concept around the old place – once described the good writer as 'neither a leader nor a follower, but a bright white golf ball in a fairway of wind-blown daisies.' In cricket, too, individuality and personality should be all; but not, alas, in the modern English game. It's sad to think that many of the prominent players whose deeds feature in these pages would not, in all probability, last five minutes at a twenty-first century county club. Colin Milburn and 'Bumper' Wells? Too fat. Joe Potter, Fred Bakewell and 'Nobby' Clark? Too nonconformist. George Thompson and Brian Reynolds? Not mercenary enough. Lifestyle issues, the dress code (Charlie Pool's boater and Freddie Brown's Quidnuncs cap?) and presence of facial hair would rule out any number of others.

But in the fervent hope that first-class cricket at Northampton will survive the bloodthirsty efforts of the 'streamliners' who would gladly dance a jig on the graves of the smaller counties, I would like to dedicate this book to Northamptonshire's cricketers of the future – especially the home-grown ones. May they play their part in victories worthy of inclusion in an updated edition, a few years down the line.

Andrew Radd
February 2002

THE 50 CLASSIC MATCHES

1882	v. Australians	Northampton	Tourist Match
1886	v. Surrey Club & Ground	Northampton	Friendly
1900	v. M.C.C. & Ground	Lord's	Friendly
1904	v. Staffordshire	Stoke-on-Trent	Minor Counties
1905	v. Derbyshire	Northampton	Championship
1906	v. Worcestershire	Worcester	Championship
1910	v. Yorkshire	Sheffield	Championship
1912	v. Surrey	Northampton	Championship
1914	v. Leicestershire	Northampton	Championship
1921	v. Essex	Northampton	Championship
1925	v. Worcestershire	Kidderminster	Championship
1929	v. Kent	Northampton	Championship
1930	v. Australians	Northampton	Tourist Match
1933	v. West Indians	Northampton	Tourist Match
1935	v. Somerset	Taunton	Championship
1939	v. Leicestershire	Northampton	Championship
1947	v. Leicestershire	Leicester	Championship
1949	v. Somerset	Taunton	Championship
1952	v. Indians	Northampton	Tourist Match
1953	v. Lancashire	Old Trafford	Championship
1955	v. Essex	Wellingborough	Championship
1957	v. Surrey	The Oval	Championship
1958	v. Yorkshire	Northampton	Championship
1961	v. Australians	Northampton	Tourist Match
1963	v. Sussex	Northampton	Gillette Cup
1965	v. Glamorgan	Cardiff	Championship
1966	v. Essex	Clacton-on-sea	Championship
1969	v. West Indians	Northampton	Tourist Match
1972	v. Australians	Northampton	Tourist Match
1974	v. Lancashire	Northampton	Sunday League
1974	v. Essex	Leyton	Championship
1976	v. Lancashire	Lord's	Gillette Cup
1979	v. Sussex	Hove	Gillette Cup
1980	v. Essex	Lord's	B & H Cup
1981	v. Lancashire	Northampton	NatWest Trophy
1981	v. Derbyshire	Lord's	NatWest Trophy
1982	v. Derbyshire	Northampton	Championship
1985	v. Surrey	Guildford	Sunday League
1986	v. Sussex	Hastings	Championship
1987	v. Kent	Canterbury	B & H Cup
1987	v. Yorkshire	Northampton	Championship
1988	v. Warwickshire	Northampton	Championship
1990	v. Hampshire	Southampton	NatWest Trophy
1992	v. Leicestershire	Lord's	NatWest Trophy
1995	v. Warwickshire	Edgbaston	Championship
1995	v. Nottinghamshire	Northampton	Championship
1996	v. Warwickshire	Northampton	B & H Cup
1998	v. Glamorgan	Northampton	Championship
2000	v. Gloucestershire	Northampton	Championship
2001	v. Essex	Northampton	Championship

THE AUSTRALIANS

3, 4 July 1882 at Northampton

The visit of Billy Murdoch's 1882 Australians presented the recently-organised Northamptonshire County Cricket Club with its biggest challenge to date, both on and off the field. Four years earlier, in July 1878, the county's most prominent cricketing gentlemen had gathered to discuss 'the best means of placing (Northamptonshire) on a footing of equality with other counties.' A new committee was elected with the fifth Earl Spencer – a notable figure in successive Gladstone governments – as president and the energetic Fred Tebbutt as secretary. Now they faced the task of handling all the arrangements for an 'international' fixture on Northampton Racecourse.

Everyone was mindful of the shambles in June 1880 when the previous touring side under Murdoch's captaincy had been invited (by a group of individuals from the town rather than the county club) to tackle Eighteen of Northampton at St James's End – later Franklin's Gardens, home of Northampton Saints RFC – in direct competition to Northamptonshire's 'official' game on the Racecourse, against Hertfordshire.

Thankfully, there was no counter-attraction this time. The club charged the vendors of refreshments and souvenirs to trade in the ground, approximately 10,000 spectators turned up over the two days, and even after forking out five guineas to the Freemen of the Borough for the privilege of enclosing what was at other times a public right of way – not to mention a few shillings for coloured ribbons to mark out club officials – the final balance sheet showed a surplus of £97. And the match itself wasn't even much of a contest.

The Northamptonshire side represented a cross-section of Victorian society. It included one 'mercenary' in the Nottinghamshire and England bowler, Alfred Shaw, whose performance scarcely merited his £10 match fee, plus two other professional trundlers, Tom Bowley and the bibulous Tom Alley. There were three members of the remarkable Kingston family – Fred, Jim (the captain) and Harry – and the brothers Pigg, Herbert and Charles – also nicknamed 'Hot' and 'Cold.' The Reverend Henry St John Reade, nephew of the novelist Charles Reade, was the headmaster of Oundle School, and another clergyman, R.F. Winch, one of his masters. John Furley, an amateur from Oakham, completed the team.

Gallant chaps all, but no match for the 'Cornstalks'. Fred Spofforth, George Palmer and Tom Garrett shared the wickets, while the mighty George Bonnor delighted the crowd with some of his trademark big hits. The tourists completed a comfortable victory just as rain began to fall, and a few weeks later made history with their seven-run triumph over England at The Oval, thus triggering a long-standing and occasionally acrimonious dispute as to who should hold the ashes of English cricket. A matter of trifling importance to secretary Tebbutt, however, compared with a £97 deposit in Northamptonshire's bank account.

The organiser – Fred Tebbutt, Northamptonshire's honorary secretary from 1878 to 1883.

Northamptonshire won the toss and elected to bat

Umpires: Not Known

NORTHAMPTONSHIRE

J Furley	b Spofforth	9		c Spofforth b Palmer	10
FW Kingston+	b Palmer	2	(7)	not out	3
JP Kingston*	b Spofforth	4		b Spofforth	0
H Pigg	c&b Garrett	26		b Palmer	22
C Pigg	c Murdoch b Garrett	17		c Beal b Palmer	24
HJ Kingston	st Murdoch b Garrett	2	(9)	b Palmer	0
T Bowley	b Garrett	0	(8)	b Palmer	0
A Shaw	not out	22	(2)	b Spofforth	0
RF Winch	b Palmer	15	(6)	run out	2
HStJ Reade	b Spofforth	5		b Palmer	0
T Alley	b Palmer	1		c Bannerman b Garrett	0
Extras		19			7
TOTAL		122			68

FOW 1st: 15,15,22,65,70,70,82,101,117
FOW 2nd: 0,0,12,57,63,65,65,65,65

Bowling 1st: Spofforth 18-7-32-3 Palmer 20.3-9-34-4 Garrett 14-3-27-3 Giffen 11-6-10-0

Bowling 2nd: Spofforth 14-3-35-2 Palmer 18-9-22-6 Garrett 4.1-2-4-1

AUSTRALIANS

WL Murdoch*+	c Shaw b Alley	15
AC Bannerman	c HJ Kingston b Bowley	17
TP Horan	c C Pigg b Alley	10
PS McDonnell	b Furley	38
G Giffen	b Bowley	51
GJ Bonnor	run out	58
SP Jones	b Shaw	5
TW Garrett	b Winch	32
FR Spofforth	b Bowley	1
GE Palmer	not out	20
CW Beal	b Winch	0
Extras		23
TOTAL		270

FOW 1st: 17,33,71,104,197,214,217,218,270

Bowling 1st: Shaw 57-34-58-1 Alley 43-13-84-2 Bowley 28-10-59-3 JP Kingston 2-0-11-0 Furley 11-1-28-1 Winch 7-3-7-2 H Pigg 1-1-0-0

AUSTRALIANS WON BY AN INNINGS AND 80 RUNS

SURREY CLUB AND GROUND
14, 15 May 1886 at Northampton

Northamptonshire's days of staging their home matches on a cricket ground across which the general public – and, once, a heavy horse and brewer's dray – could trample, came to an end in the spring of 1886 when the club played its first game on the brand new County Ground. The ten-acre site, between Abington Lane and Wellingborough Road, had been approved at a special meeting of members in November 1884, and capital was raised by the sale of £5 shares in the Northampton County Cricket and Recreation Grounds Company. Architect James Ingman's plans for a pavilion 'of red brick, with a roof of blue slates ornamented with a bell turret … and a splendid well of water at the rear' became reality in the winter of 1885/86. Thoughts then turned to the opening fixture. Thomas Henry Vials, who succeeded Fred Tebbutt as secretary in 1883, tried unsuccessfully to get the Australians to come. Instead, a two-day game was arranged against Surrey Club and Ground.

The heavens did not smile on Northamptonshire's great day; indeed, they opened to such miserable effect that no play at all was possible on the Friday. Saturday dawned bright but bitterly cold, and only a smattering of hardy spectators witnessed Fred Kingston (a high-minded parson, whose 1888 offering *Cedric, or A Soul's Travail*, in which the eponymous hero converses with the spirit of the recently-martyred General Gordon, was not a best-seller) face the inaugural delivery from Surrey's steady left-armer, Edward D'Oyley Barratt, at half-past-eleven. Reduced admission prices after lunch and the factory workers' half-holiday drew several hundred more sensation-seekers through the gates (in the charge of bristling ex-Colour Sergeant Newling, appointed to keep out ne'er-do-wells) during the afternoon, but it was undeniably a quiet and low-key christening.

Northamptonshire's cricket reflected, by and large, the cheerless conditions. Only G.H. – Bert – Kingston (who lived until 1959, the last survivor of the nine brothers) prospered with the bat, hitting a spirited unbeaten 40. His father, William Kingston senior, proposed a toast to the new ground during luncheon (taken with the county in trouble at 99 for eight), and the response came from Surrey's captain, Monty Bowden, who then went out and scored the venue's maiden half-century.

Joe Potter was a well-travelled and – according to James Lillywhite's *Annual* – 'still very puzzling' old bowler, whose up-and-down relationship with Northamptonshire encompassed plenty of overs, plenty of wickets and at least one threat of legal action for non-payment of wages. He made his own mark on the occasion by claiming the wicket of Fred Bush with his first ball, brilliantly caught one-handed by Jim Kingston at point. But he blotted his copybook by dropping Bowden at slip off Tom Beale's leg-spin, and the Surrey skipper celebrated by hoisting Potter over long-on for the ground's very first six – a carry of 125 yards, according to contemporary reports.

The remarkable Kingston family. The nine brothers are, from left to right, back row: C.A. (Charles), W.P. (Walter), G.H. (Bert), W.H. (Billy), H.E. (Tim). Seated: H.J. (Harold), F.W. (Fred), J.P. (Jim). On ground: F.C. (Frank). Of the nine, only Frank did not play for the county.

Surrey v. Northamptonshire

Northamptonshire won the toss and elected to bat

Umpires: Not Known

NORTHAMPTONSHIRE

FW Kingston+	b Shacklock	15
TG Beale	b Shacklock	5
JB Challen	lbw b Shacklock	4
GH Kingston	not out	40
WP Kingston	c&b Shacklock	6
JP Kingston*	c EA Bush b FW Bush	2
C Bull	b Shacklock	14
RF Winch	b Shacklock	9
T Lowe	c&b Brockwell	7
J Potter	c EA Bush b Brockwell	1
T Alley	b Brockwell	0
Extras	(b3 lb1)	4
TOTAL		107

FOW 1st: Not known

Bowling 1st: Barratt 39-20-39-0 Shacklock 38-19-39-6 FW Bush 9-5-10-1 Lockyer 3-0-10-0 Henderson 4-2-3-0 Brockwell 11-9-2-3

SURREY CLUB AND GROUND

FW Bush	c JP Kingston b Potter	0
W Brockwell	b Lowe	9
EJ Diver	st FW Kingston b Beale	27
EA Bush+	b Lowe	0
MP Bowden*	not out	50
R Henderson	not out	25
F Shacklock		
F Abraham		
J Lockyer		
R Voss		
E Barratt		
Extras	(lb3)	3
TOTAL	(4 wkts)	114

FOW 1st: Not known

Bowling: Potter 29-8-33-1 Alley 19-8-22-0 Beale 18-3-33-1 Lowe 24-15-23-2

MATCH DRAWN

MCC

While the rest of the nation fretted over the fate of plucky Colonel Baden-Powell and his comrades, besieged by the Boers in Mafeking since the previous October, Tom Horton's Northamptonshire team underlined its growing reputation with a magnificent performance on the grandest cricketing stage of all. It was not the county's first win at headquarters, nor was the opposition especially formidable, but the ten-wicket triumph – and, more significantly, the manner of achieving it – lent added weight to the view that Northamptonshire would be leaving behind second-class cricket sooner rather than later.

Three players dominated proceedings: two home-grown professionals, George Thompson and Billy East, and a home-grown amateur, one Lancelot Townshend Driffield. If Thompson is the finest all-round cricketer Northamptonshire has ever produced – and few would or could dispute that – then East was his doughty partner in a highly productive double act for the best part of two decades. Horton always maintained that the pair made captaincy a simple exercise: 'I started with Thompson and East, and then switched to East and Thompson!'

Driffield's career was altogether briefer. A vicar's son from the village of Old, he made his Northamptonshire debut as a schoolboy in 1898, won a blue at Cambridge four years later and appeared spasmodically for the county until 1908. This was, perhaps, his finest hour. Against an attack carried by three Leicestershire professionals – Arthur Woodcock, Dick Pougher and Fred Geeson – the left-handed Driffield helped Thompson add 190 for the second wicket, nearly all those runs coming before lunch on the first day. As the *Northampton Mercury* observed: 'The MCC captain seemed almost at a loss to know what to do.'

Wicketkeeper Charlie Smith, an erratic but occasionally effective batsman, enlivened the latter stages of the innings with a typically idiosyncratic 57, and Thompson was left unbeaten on 186 not out, his highest score for the county. Having carried his bat, he was then called upon to open the bowling and, not surprisingly, led off with four weary wides before finding his direction. Next day, Thompson and East shared 17 of the 20 wickets as MCC were dismissed twice, leaving Horton and Smith to complete the formalities.

And there was better to come. Returning from London that Friday evening, the players would have arrived back in Northampton just in time to hear the town's mayor announce from the balcony of the Guildhall that Mafeking had been relieved. A.J. 'Pat' Darnell, Northamptonshire's honorary secretary from 1898 to 1921, let off some celebratory fireworks at his local Conservative club; a neighbour, assuming the place was going up in flames, called out the fire brigade.

Lancelot Townshend Driffield played the innings of his life against MCC at Lord's in 1900, aged just nineteen.

Northamptonshire won the toss and elected to bat

Umpires: Not known

NORTHAMPTONSHIRE

T Horton*	c Oates b Woodcock	7		not out	15
GJ Thompson	not out	186			
WH Kingston	b Woodcock	0			
LT Driffield	b Woodcock	109			
W East	lbw b Geeson	13			
GH Colson	b Woodcock	0			
HE Kingston	st Oates b Geeson	1			
RF Knight	c Geeson b Pougher	23			
KC Craig	c Woodcock b Pougher	7			
BC Smith+	b Pougher	57	(2)	not out	13
M Cox	c&b Pougher	20			
Extras		6			1
TOTAL		429		(0 wkt)	29

FOW 1st: Not known

Bowling 1st: Woodcock 42-8-128-4 Geeson 45-9-132-2 Pougher 36.1-13-110-4
Somerset 4-1-20-0 Page 7-0-33-0

Bowling 2nd: Woodcock 2-0-13-0 Geeson 1.2-0-15-0

MCC AND GROUND

DC Lee	b Thompson	7	c WH Kingston b Thompson	0
AH Hornby	c HE Kingston b Thompson	48	b Thompson	25
AF Somerset	c WH Kingston b Thompson	20	c Smith b East	45
BV Wentworth	b East	51	c Smith b East	8
A Page	c Colson b Driffield	2	c Colson b Thompson	35
CE Greenway	c Driffield b Thompson	4	c Horton b HE Kingston	21
AD Pougher	not out	85	c Knight b East	0
RL Crankshaw	b Cox	0	b Thompson	36
F Geeson	c Smith b East	1	not out	12
TW Oates+	b East	15	b East	2
A Woodcock	b East	1	b East	8
Extras		12		18
TOTAL		246		210

FOW 1st: Not known
FOW 2nd: Not known

Bowling 1st: Thompson 19-1-56-4 Cox 10-0-40-1 Driffield 10-1-26-1 HE Kingston
10-0-55-0 East 14.1-2-57-4

Bowling 2nd: Thompson 23-5-71-4 Driffield 5-0-18-0 HE Kingston 6-0-50-1 East
21.2-6-53-5

NORTHAMPTONSHIRE WON BY 10 WICKETS

STAFFORDSHIRE

4, 5 July 1904 at Stoke-on-Trent

Sydney Francis Barnes is still acknowledged, nearly ninety years after his final Test appearance, as one of the greatest bowlers in cricket history. His record at international level is simply breathtaking: a tally of 189 wickets in 27 games at 16.43 runs apiece. In all competitive cricket, he is reckoned to have dismissed more than 6,000 batsmen with a single-figure average. But he met his match one day in July 1904, thwarted by a Northampton sports outfitter named Billy Kingston.

Northamptonshire carried off the Minor Counties title in 1903 and began their defence the following season with three victories, the first of them by an innings and 159 runs over Staffordshire at the County Ground. George Thompson's contribution to that thumping win was 83 and nine wickets, but he was missing for the return fixture, having 'ricked himself' the previous week. The other major talking point was the earth tremor that shook Stoke the day before the match. Whether as a consequence of that seismic disturbance or not, the pitch originally prepared was found to be too uneven when the captains inspected it on the first morning. A new one was cut out but, according to the *Northampton Daily Reporter*, 'it did not wear well.'

Henry Hawkins – a fast bowling, fox hunting amateur from Everdon Hall – took the new ball in Thompson's absence, and shared the honours with East as the home side were dismissed by mid-afternoon. Then it was Barnes' turn. Neville Cardus detected 'a Mephistophelian aspect about him', and he must indeed have appeared as the devil incarnate to Northamptonshire's batsmen who, with the exception of Eddie Crosse, shaped poorly. Staffordshire led by 52, only to struggle themselves against the lively pace of Hawkins and East's metronomic control. The visitors went in again needing 161 in three hours on this under-prepared and rapidly deteriorating track.

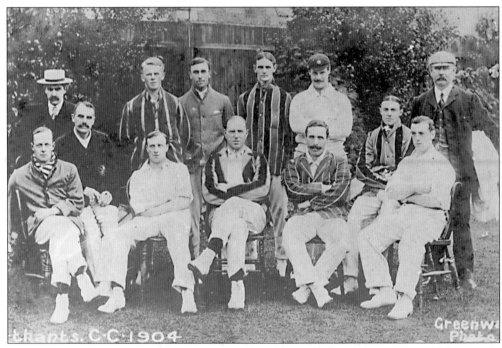

Northamptonshire, 1904 – the club's final season as a minor county. From left to right, standing: L. Bullimer (scorer), C.R. Wetherall, M. Cox, H.H.K. Worsley, W. East, A. Stockwin (umpire). Seated: H.B Simpson, B.C. Smith, W.H. Kingston, T. Horton (captain), G.J. Thompson, E.M. Crosse, R.F. Knight.

Kingston, the second-youngest of the brothers, decided that attack was the wisest policy. He and Tom Horton put on 109 for the first wicket in only eighty minutes, and Kingston – who owned a sports shop in Northampton for many years – hammered 102 out of 150, with a five and eight fours, before chipping Barnes to mid-on. Four more wickets then fell quickly as Staffordshire hit back, but Hawkins and 'Bumper' Wells saw Northamptonshire to their target. It had been, the *Reporter* reckoned, 'one of the most exciting finishes in second-class cricket for many a long day.'

Billy Kingston's immediate reward was selection for the Gentlemen against the Players at The Oval later that week. The Gents won easily but, cricket being the great leveller, the county's representative was bowled by Warwickshire's Sam Hargreave for 5. Sadly for Kingston, S.F. Barnes wasn't playing.

COUNTY CRICKETERS.

W.H. Kingston.

Eddie Crosse.

COUNTY CRICKETERS.

MR. E. M. CROSSE,
NORTHAMPTONSHIRE.

COUNTY CRICKETERS.

MR. H. HAWKINS,
NORTHAMPTONSHIRE.

Henry Hawkins.

Staffordshire won the toss and elected to bat

Umpires: Not known

STAFFORDSHIRE

Brown	c Shaw b Wells	39	c Wells b East	4
J Fereday	c&b Hawkins	17	not out	46
SF Barnes	c Wetherall b East	13	c Wells b East	1
Hollowood	b Edwards	27	c Kingston b East	0
HD Stratton	b East	12	b Hawkins	17
GW Crane	c Wells b East	37	c Horton b East	10
H Bagland	lbw b Hawkins	37	c Kingston b Hawkins	6
B Meakin	not out	15	b Hawkins	4
J Poole+	c Crosse b Hawkins	0	b Hawkins	9
C Goodall	run out	0	b East	0
TA Grose	b Wells	0	b East	0
Extras		11		11
TOTAL		208		108

FOW 1st: 52,62,100,100,136,151,199,199,199
FOW 2nd: 11,15,15,49,62,82,86,107,108

Bowling 1st: Hawkins 12-3-27-3 Edwards 16-2-73-1 East 21-3-56-3 Wells 11.3-0-41-2

Bowling 2nd: East 22.5-10-32-6 Edwards 8-1-17-0 Hawkins 19-4-33-4 Cox 5-2-15-0

NORTHAMPTONSHIRE

WH Kingston	c Hollowood b Barnes	14	c Goodall b Barnes	102
EM Crosse	c Brown b Barnes	45		
M Cox	b Crane	14	c Poole b Barnes	3
GAT Vials	b Crane	10 (5)	b Goodall	1
W East	b Barnes	13 (4)	b Barnes	4
T Horton*	not out	27 (2)	b Fereday	35
AS Wetherall	b Barnes	4 (6)	c Poole b Goodall	0
J Shaw	c Hollowood b Barnes	7 (7)	b Goodall	0
H Hawkins	c&b Brown	1 (8)	not out	3
W Wells	c Poole b Barnes	5 (9)	not out	2
WH Edwards	b Barnes	12		
Extras		4		12
TOTAL		156	(7 wkts)	162

FOW 1st: 29,56,72,86,100,109,119,127,144
FOW 2nd: 109,144,150,155,157,157,159

Bowling 1st: Barnes 29.2-8-72-7 Goodall 19-3-47-0 Crane 11-3-25-2 Grose 1-0-5-0 Brown 1-0-3-1

Bowling 2nd: Barnes 19-3-62-4 Crane 3-0-16-0 Fereday 9-1-37-1 Goodall 9-5-18-2 Brown 1-0-7-0 Meakin 2-0-10-0

NORTHAMPTONSHIRE WON BY 3 WICKETS

DERBYSHIRE

19, 20, 21 June 1905 at Northampton

It wasn't long before the optimism and ballyhoo that surrounded Northamptonshire's elevation to first-class status in the winter of 1904/05 gave way to cold realism. So much depended on George Thompson; a point not lost on the pavilion and press-box wags who amused themselves by dubbing the newcomers 'Thompsonshire.' It was hard for county supporters to see the joke. After a respectable draw with Hampshire in the opening fixture at Southampton, Tom Horton's men had been trounced twice by Sussex, at Hove and Northampton, with a near wash-out against Leicestershire in between.

Northamptonshire owed their next opponents, Derbyshire, a considerable debt of gratitude. When 'Pat' Darnell was assembling the club's first County Championship programme – six opposing teams, home and away, were needed to meet the minimum requirement as laid down at a meeting of secretaries in December 1904 – it was 'The Peakites' who stepped in to complete the list. It was a noble gesture, and much good did it do them.

Charlie Pool, the elegant amateur who had scored Northamptonshire's maiden century in the Minor Counties competition in 1896 and was to do the same at first-class level in the return against Hampshire a couple of weeks after this game, gave his side a promising start. He was unbeaten on 48 at lunch, only to be run out immediately afterwards without addition. His departure triggered a dismal collapse as the last seven wickets fell for 58, but Derbyshire followed suit after a delayed start on the second day, Thompson and Billy East reducing them from 138 for three overnight to 177 all out.

By now, the bowlers were firmly in charge. No one reached 30 in Northamptonshire's second effort, interrupted by more rain, and the visitors went in again just before one o'clock on the final afternoon needing 124 to win. Thompson and East removed four men for 58 in the pre-lunch session, then proceeded to work their way through the rest. Word got around, and the new electric trams – introduced into the town the previous summer – carried a healthy number of spectators to the ground, all eager to see history made. It duly was, at five minutes to four.

'We had succeeded in wooing cricket's goddess, we had crested Derbyshire's peaks,' wrote the *Northampton Independent*'s sporting columnist, 'Veteran'. 'We had put up the number one victory of Northamptonshire in first-class cricket, and to us was the joy, the honour and the glory.' To Thompson, East and their fellow professionals came a more tangible reward in the form of £10 from one of the club's most generous patrons, Wentworth Vernon, who had saved Northamptonshire's blushes a few years earlier by covering the wage bill when the bank refused to extend the overdraft in mid-season. 'Veteran' may have gone a touch over the top, but it was still a result to relish.

George Thompson.

Northamptonshire won the toss and elected to bat

Umpires: RG Barlow & CE Richardson

NORTHAMPTONSHIRE

WH Kingston	c Humphries b Warren	2		c Ollivierre b Warren	13
GJ Thompson	lbw b Bestwick	15	(5)	c Lawton b Cupitt	8
CJT Pool	run out	48	(2)	c Ollivierre b Morton	23
M Cox	c Bestwick b Cadman	14	(3)	c Wright b Morton	10
W East	b Bestwick	11	(6)	b Warren	12
EM Crosse	b Bestwick	12	(4)	c Cadman b Morton	28
HE Kingston	not out	26		not out	17
GAT Vials	b Bestwick	4		c Storer b Bestwick	8
T Horton*	run out	5		st Humphries b Bestwick	0
H Hawkins	c Humphries b Storer	0		b Bestwick	4
BC Smith+	c Wright b Storer	9		c Humphries b Cupitt	5
Extras	(b8 lb4 nb2)	14		(b8 nb4)	12
TOTAL		160			140

FOW 1st: 7,39,88,102,104,115,121,142,142
FOW 2nd: 33,45,49,84,89,104,127,127,135

Bowling 1st: Cadman 10-5-17-1 Warren 6-1-7-1 Cupitt 20-10-34-0 Bestwick 22-8-47-4 Morton 7-2-24-0 Lawton 2-1-8-0 Storer 3.3-0-9-2

DERBYSHIRE

LG Wright	c WH Kingston b East	12		c Hawkins b Thompson	25
CA Ollivierre	b Thompson	0		c Vials b East	17
A Morton	c Smith b Hawkins	30		b Thompson	0
GR Sparrow	c Vials b Thompson	64	(5)	c Vials b East	5
AE Lawton*	run out	40	(7)	c HE Kingston b East	11
W Storer	c WH Kingston b Thompson	10	(4)	b East	9
AR Warren	c HE Kingston b Thompson	8	(6)	b Thompson	4
SWA Cadman	b East	5		not out	12
J Humphries+	c Thompson b East	0		lbw b East	0
J Cupitt	not out	0		b East	1
W Bestwick	c Hawkins b Thompson	0		b Thompson	1
Extras	(b6 lb1 nb1)	8		(b5 lb4 nb6)	15
TOTAL		177			100

FOW 1st: 1,15,85,149,153,163,175,177,177
FOW 2nd: 45,45,51,58,75,83,85,85,95

Bowling 1st: Thompson 25.2-2-66-5 East 21-4-47-3 Cox 9-2-29-0 Pool 2-0-9-0 Hawkins 6-2-18-1

Bowling 2nd: Thompson 22.4-8-52-4 East 22-9-33-6

NORTHAMPTONSHIRE WON BY 23 RUNS

WORCESTERSHIRE

10, 11, 12 May 1906 at Worcester

Worcester's most famous son, Sir Edward Elgar, was out of the country in the spring of 1906, on a conducting tour in the United States. Accordingly, Northamptonshire's stunning victory after following on against his native county must have escaped the great man's notice. Had it not, he would surely have tacked a couple of cryptically-initialled movements on to his Enigma Variations – 'C.J.T.P.' and 'G.J.T.'

The cathedral bell was chiming midday as Worcestershire launched their innings on a chilly May day and, despite more heroics from George Thompson – eight for 92, with Billy East proving uncharacteristically expensive on this occasion – the home side put up a useful-looking score. Just how useful became apparent by the close, which arrived with Northamptonshire in deep trouble at 86 for seven in reply. A quarter-of-an-hour sufficed for Ted Arnold and George Wilson to tidy up next morning, and Reginald Brinton – leading Worcestershire in the absence of Harry Foster – sent the opposition in again, 165 runs adrift. This decision was to backfire in spectacular fashion.

Charlie Pool had been Northamptonshire's leading light with the bat during their debut first-class season in 1905, and even inspired a lengthy poem (of sorts) in *Athletic News*: 'When the bowlers find a spot/And they're serving things up hot/When there setteth in a rot/Send for Pool!' And so on, for another seven verses. The rot had well and truly set in this time, and when he went to the crease at three o'clock on the second afternoon, the county still needed a further 34 to avoid losing by an innings, with two wickets down.

Pool's polished and wristy style made him a firm favourite with both spectators and reporters ('There is no more delightful sight … than watching the slim, athletic form of Mr C.J.T. Pool at the wickets, gathering runs as easily as blackberries … ') and in three hours he cut and drove his way to a memorable and chanceless 166, turning the match on its head. Northamptonshire ended the day on 379 for seven, a lead of 214, and first thing on Saturday they extended their advantage to 253. Instead of enjoying a day off, Worcestershire found themselves facing a testing task in the fourth innings, albeit on a pitch still good for batting.

They were in reasonable shape on 95 for two at lunch, but Thompson, with his whirling, windmill-like action, destroyed the middle order. Only the Australian, Jack Cuffe, offered any serious resistance with a brave 76, and by five o'clock Northamptonshire's players were putting their feet up after securing what must still be regarded as one of the county's unlikeliest wins. Pool and Thompson were the heroes, leaving even the *Athletic News* versifier – mercifully – lost for words.

COUNTY CRICKETERS.

MR. C. J. T. POOL,

Charlie Pool.

Worcestershire won the toss and elected to bat

Umpires: RG Barlow & AE Clapp

WORCESTERSHIRE

FL Bowley	b Thompson	85	b Thompson		11
RS Brinton*	b Thompson	1	c Smith b Wells		26
EG Arnold	b Baker	39	c Smith b Thompson		7
WB Burns	b Thompson	2	lbw b Thompson		24
JA Cuffe	lbw b Thompson	41	c Baker b Thompson		76
GF Wheldon	c Wells b Baker	22	b Thompson		0
GW Gaukrodger+	c Baker b Thompson	4	c Smith b Baker		0
RD Burrows	b Thompson	16	b Baker		15
A Bird	not out	10	b Thompson		26
GA Wilson	b Thompson	28	c Horton b East		9
EW Solly	c Horton b Thompson	2	not out		0
Extras	(b9 lb2 nb5)	16	(b9 nb9)		18
TOTAL		266			212

FOW 1st: 7,127,129,129,192,203,208,?,?
FOW 2nd: 17,73,124,139,139,145,162,192,211

Bowling 1st: Thompson 34.4-5-92-8 East 18-1-66-0 Cox 8-1-24-0 Wells 4-0-14-0 Baker 14-3-54-2

Bowling 2nd: Thompson 34.3-5-72-6 East 20-4-64-1 Wells 6-2-12-1 Baker 12-2-38-2 HE Kingston 4-1-8-0

NORTHAMPTONSHIRE

T Horton*	b Wilson	2 (6)	b Burrows		2
WH Kingston	b Arnold	21 (3)	b Burrows		61
CJT Pool	b Arnold	12 (4)	c Gaukrodger b Bird		166
HE Kingston	b Arnold	0 (8)	c Gaukrodger b Arnold		28
GAT Vials	lbw b Arnold	5 (7)	lbw b Wilson		14
GJ Thompson	c Gaukrodger b Arnold	14 (5)	b Cuffe		24
W East	lbw b Arnold	4 (9)	b Arnold		18
M Cox	not out	28 (2)	b Wilson		72
C Baker	c Gaukrodger b Arnold	3 (10)	b Wilson		1
W Wells	c Gaukrodger b Wilson	5 (11)	not out		0
BC Smith+	lbw b Arnold	3 (1)	b Cuffe		12
Extras	(b1 lb3)	4	(b10 lb8 nb2)		20
TOTAL		101			418

FOW 1st: 8,25,25,33,55,56,69,79,94
FOW 2nd: 21,131,182,324,?,?,397,412,?,418

Bowling 1st: Wilson 19-4-40-2 Arnold 23.1-10-46-8 Cuffe 5-1-11-0

Bowling 2nd: Wilson 30.4-4-98-3 Arnold 32-8-81-2 Cuffe 25-6-71-2 Bird 21-4-56-1 Burrows 23-4-67-2 Solly 8-2-25-0

NORTHAMPTONSHIRE WON BY 41 RUNS

YORKSHIRE

20, 21, 22 June 1910 at Sheffield

Yorkshire did not appear on Northamptonshire's first three County Championship fixture lists. The sides met for the first time at Northampton in 1908, and the Tykes won without breaking sweat, dismissing their lowly hosts for 27 and 15. Although Charlie Pool and Billy East were both missing and George Thompson couldn't contribute after being struck down with a bad back during the match, it was all deeply embarrassing. The second-innings performance appeared as something other than a complete disaster only when set against the 12 all out at Gloucester a year earlier.

For the straw-clutchers among the Northamptonshire faithful, there was at least one encouraging omen as the team headed up to Bramall Lane in 1910. When Lancashire visited the County Ground in 1908 – barely three weeks after the Yorkshire debacle – Charlie Pool deputised for 'Tim' Manning as captain, and Northamptonshire triumphed by one wicket in a thrilling finish. Now, Pool was in charge again, with Manning a victim of lumbago.

Yorkshire shaded the first day's honours thanks largely to an aggressive, if chancy, innings from David Denton. Northamptonshire lost Pool early next morning, edging to slip, and that brought 'Tubby' Vials to the crease. Vials, a Northampton solicitor and son of the club's former honorary secretary, made his county debut in 1904 and remained closely connected with Northamptonshire – as player, captain, committee member, chairman and president – until 1968. A doubtful starter for this match, troubled by a recurring knee injury, he gritted his teeth and clouted George Hirst for three boundaries in an over on his way to an invaluable century in three-and-a-quarter hours.

Vials and Sydney Smith, Trinidad-born of Anglo-Scottish parentage and impressing many good judges in only his second full season in England, helped Northamptonshire to 229 for four, only for the last six wickets to add only eight runs. Yorkshire went in again 51 to the good, but

Thompson and Daventry's 'Bumper' Wells wrought havoc in an eventful final session and the home side were all out for 132 at the close. Twenty wickets had fallen in the day, leaving Northamptonshire to score 184 for victory.

'Will Northamptonshire Win?' asked the *Daily Echo*, and attempted to provide the answer by quoting an anonymous county player: 'We ought to get the runs, but you know what an extraordinary side we are.' Indeed. When Smith holed out at deep square leg off Wilfred Rhodes, the scoreboard read 66 for four, and the issue was very much in the balance. But the ever-reliable Thompson found a willing partner in Bob Haywood, a product of the famous Tonbridge nursery, and together they ushered Northamptonshire to their target with five wickets in hand. Yorkshire had been beaten for the first time. It was, according to the *Echo*, 'quite the best thing Northamptonshire has done in cricket.' The new boys' inferiority complex was being slowly but surely overcome.

G.A.T. 'Tubby' Vials.

Yorkshire won the toss and elected to bat

Umpires: RG Barlow & JE West

YORKSHIRE

W Rhodes	b Thompson	56	b Thompson	0
JW Rothery	b Wells	1	b Wells	1
D Denton	b Wells	70	c Ellis b Wells	7
WH Wilkinson	lbw b Smith	37	b Wells	21
GH Hirst	c Vials b Thompson	26	b Wells	0
H Myers	lbw b Thompson	0	st Ellis b East	21
A Drake	b East	12	c Ellis b Wells	8
EJRH Radcliffe*	b Seymour	36	c East b Smith	21
S Haigh	not out	26	not out	26
JT Newstead	c&b Seymour	4	c Haywood b Thompson	21
A Dolphin+	b Seymour	0	b Thompson	2
Extras	(b10 lb6 nb4)	20	(b2 nb2)	4
TOTAL		288		132

FOW 1st: 1,136,136,190,191,216,228,278,288
FOW 2nd: 1,1,18,18,39,51,73,95,130

Bowling 1st: Thompson 28-9-63-3 Wells 24-5-73-2 East 23-5-58-1 Smith 13-2-54-1 JS Denton 3-0-13-0 Seymour 1.5-0-7-3

Bowling 2nd: Thompson 15.4-3-37-3 Wells 13-1-44-5 East 10-5-17-1 Smith 5-0-18-1 Seymour 5-1-12-0

NORTHAMPTONSHIRE

CJT Pool*	c Hirst b Newstead	23	b Myers	3
J Seymour	b Rhodes	33	b Hirst	25
GAT Vials	c Newstead b Myers	100	b Rhodes	30
SG Smith	lbw b Myers	53	c Denton b Rhodes	7
GJ Thompson	lbw b Myers	1	not out	41
W East	c Dolphin b Myers	9	lbw b Rhodes	23
RA Haywood	c&b Hirst	2	not out	49
JS Denton	lbw b Myers	0		
WH Denton	c Haigh b Myers	0		
W Wells	b Hirst	1		
H Ellis+	not out	0		
Extras	(b11 lb4)	15	(b4 lb1 nb1)	6
TOTAL		237	(5 wkts)	184

FOW 1st: 44,79,163,167,229,234,235,236,237
FOW 2nd: 3,48,66,66,119

Bowling 1st: Hirst 18.1-6-32-2 Newstead 20-4-44-1 Drake 14-2-29-0 Rhodes 13-3-37-1 Myers 17-0-57-6 Haigh 9-3-23-0

Bowling 2nd: Hirst 10-3-21-1 Newstead 12-3-32-0 Drake 6.3-2-22-0 Rhodes 10-0-41-3 Myers 20-5-49-1 Haigh 11-2-13-0

NORTHAMPTONSHIRE WON BY 5 WICKETS

SURREY
8, 9, 10 July 1912 at Northampton

Northamptonshire surprised just about everyone in 1912, not least themselves. Using only twelve players in eighteen County Championship matches, they finished second in the table with 70.58 per cent of their possible points to Yorkshire's 72 per cent. Had it stayed fine on 7 August, when rain thwarted Northamptonshire's victory bid at Leicester and saved Yorkshire from probable defeat against Lancashire at Old Trafford, the outcome might well have been altogether more satisfactory.

'Man for man, they were not as individually gifted as, say, Kent, Lancashire or Middlesex,' observed A.A. Thomson of 'Tubby' Vials' team, 'but they had the eager and skilled cohesion of a destroyer crew under a daring and popular skipper.' In July, that cheery and determined crew sank Surrey almost without trace.

In these days of regimented preparation and fitness consultants, it is worth noting that 'Bumper' Wells – a fast bowler who subscribed to the theory that good, honest sweat needed replacing with good, honest ale – got himself into fighting trim for the Londoners' visit by turning out for the Licensed Traders of Northampton against their counterparts from North of the Thames. Wells took seven for 16 and the fixture was declared 'a great success as a social function.' He was hardly needed when Surrey batted first next day; George Thompson and the left-arm spin of Sydney Smith reduced them from 86 for one just after lunch to 95 all out, Thompson claiming the last five wickets in nine balls without conceding a run. A brief shower of rain had freshened up the pitch a little, but the collapse was still staggering.

Vials then proceeded to put the match beyond Surrey's reach with a cavalier 82 in seventy minutes, including a six and 13 fours. The explanation for this Jessopian display was as much social as tactical; the skipper was keen to get out that night to attend a friend's wedding in the morning! He was absent when Surrey went in again facing a deficit of 152, but returned from the nuptials in mid-afternoon to resume command as Ernie Hayes, assisted by the tail, saved his side from the ignominy of an innings defeat. Nevertheless, Northamptonshire needed only 91 to win and knocked them off easily, thanks to a brisk little partnership between Vials and Billy East.

It was the team's sixth victory of the season, and kept them at the head of the table. Four more wins came their way in that damp, post-*Titanic* summer, but a week after trouncing Surrey they came badly unstuck at Edgbaston against Warwickshire, the defending champions. Northamptonshire lost both the game, by 303 runs, and top spot in the Championship. They did not regain it.

A cartoonist's view of the county's surprise challenge for the 1912 County Championship title.

Surrey won the toss and elected to bat

Umpires: F Guttridge & G Webb

SURREY

MC Bird*	c Haywood b JS Denton	41	c Vials b Thompson	37
TW Hayward	c Wells b Thompson	33	c Buswell b Wells	2
EG Hayes	st Buswell b Smith	12	lbw b Smith	88
A Ducat	st Buswell b Smith	0	lbw b East	5
WA Spring	lbw b Thompson	3	b East	5
WJ Abel	st Buswell b Smith	0	b East	7
EB Myers	b Thompson	0	b Thompson	39
H Strudwick+	c Buswell b Thompson	0	b Thompson	21
EC Kirk	b Thompson	0	b Wells	21
WC Smith	c JS Denton b Smith	2	b Wells	6
T Rushby	not out	0	not out	1
Extras	(b2 w1 nb1)	4	(b3 lb1 nb6)	10
TOTAL		95		242

FOW 1st: 64,86,86,92,93,93,93,93,95
FOW 2nd: 9,66,85,102,123,174,211,222,229

Bowling 1st: Wells 6-3-5-0 Thompson 16.2-6-36-5 Smith 14-5-21-4 East 7-2-17-0
JS Denton 4-0-12-1

Bowling 2nd: Wells 22-5-63-3 Thompson 23-2-65-3 Smith 16-4-30-1 East 23-5-40-3
JS Denton 6-2-19-0 Seymour 4-1-15-0

NORTHAMPTONSHIRE

WH Denton	lbw b Smith	35	c Strudwick b Kirk	19
W East	lbw b Smith	10	not out	39
GAT Vials*	b Smith	82	not out	33
SG Smith	b Rushby	4		
GJ Thompson	b Rushby	29		
JS Denton	st Strudwick b Smith	17		
RA Haywood	b Smith	14		
J Seymour	lbw b Smith	7		
FI Walden	b Smith	30		
W Wells	not out	6		
WA Buswell+	c Strudwick b Rushby	1		
Extras	(b8 lb2 nb2)	12	(lb1)	1
TOTAL		247	(1 wkt)	92

FOW 1st: 23,120,133,133,162,184,192,228,246
FOW 2nd: 39

Bowling 1st: Smith 40-6-73-7 Rushby 23.1-6-58-3 Kirk 18-4-52-0 Hayes 5-1-34-0
Bird 3-1-18-0

Bowling 2nd: Smith 8-3-23-0 Rushby 5-1-16-0 Kirk 6-0-19-1 Myers 4.3-1-24-0
Abel 2-0-9-0

NORTHAMPTONSHIRE WON BY 9 WICKETS

LEICESTERSHIRE
3, 4, 5 August 1914 at Northampton

'The old world in its sunset was fair to see' wrote Winston Churchill, recalling the summer of 1914. While the generals consulted their railway timetables and the admirals readied their dreadnoughts, Northamptonshire's cricketers were enjoying a respectable season: seven victories and ninth place in the County Championship. It was something of a come-down after the heady days of 1912 and 1913, but it would be 1949 before they finished as high in the table again.

On the positive side, some younger players were coming to the fore. George Thompson and Billy East couldn't go on for ever, while the likes of Tom Horton, Billy Kingston and Charlie Pool had already retired. From Wellingborough School came the Denton twins, Jack and Billy, plus their younger brother Donald, and a talented all-rounder, Tommy Askham. All three Dentons turned out against Sussex at Hove, all three contributed half-centuries in Northamptonshire's 557 for six declared – a county record that would stand until 1990 – and all three appeared in the team photograph wearing their claret and white striped Wellingburian blazers. Donald was selected for The Rest against Lord's Schools at Headquarters, and so missed the next Championship match, Leicestershire's visit to the County Ground. Askham, still only seventeen, was drafted in to make his first-class debut.

Northamptonshire struggled on the Monday morning, and although Askham shared a last-wicket stand of 35 with wicketkeeper Walter Buswell, the county's 135 all out was well short of expectations. Jack King's 'seen-it-all-before' century gave Leicestershire a 93-run advantage on first innings, despite another wholehearted bowling effort from 'Bumper' Wells, who then demonstrated his batting prowess by adding 76 vital runs with the captain, Sydney Smith. Nevertheless, the visitors went in on Tuesday evening requiring only 84 to win. They lost three wickets for 13 before the close, and there would be everything to play for on the final day.

A view of the County Ground at Northampton, just before the First World War.

By the time the players re-convened on Wednesday 5 August, Great Britain was at war with Germany. The ultimatum to the Kaiser had expired at 11 p.m. the night before, and the local press was highly critical of the 'drunken patriots … the gangs of men and hobbledehoys staggering about the street' when the news filtered through to Northampton. The game went on, although one of Leicestershire's players, Aubrey Sharp, was obliged to rejoin his regiment and thus forego the dubious privilege of facing Thompson on a wearing pitch. He and East ran through the rest following a delayed start, and the 'Steelbacks' had seen off the 'Woollybacks' in a gripping finale by four runs.

A few of the spectators were astonished that Sharp had to leave there and then, rather than doing a Sir Francis Drake and finishing

The Denton twins, Billy (left) and Jack.

the game first. 'You'll be back in a fortnight,' some of them shouted. Not so. Among Northamptonshire's casualties during the next four bloody years were Askham, killed in action aged nineteen, and Don Denton, who had part of a leg amputated. The bright hopes of August 1914 were cruelly dashed, at the County Ground as elsewhere.

Sydney Smith, who played a vital innings in Northamptonshire's 1914 victory over Leicestershire at Northampton.

William 'Bumper' Wells.

Northamptonshire won the toss and elected to bat

Umpires: RG Barlow & W Richards

NORTHAMPTONSHIRE

JS Denton	b Skelding	0	c Sidwell b Skelding	4
WH Denton	b Geary	6	b Brown	5
RA Haywood	c Sharp b Brown	26	b Brown	8
SG Smith*	c Skelding b Geary	7	c Brown b Geary	74
GJ Thompson	c&b Brown	0	c Whitehead b Skelding	4
GAT Vials	lbw b Brown	34	b Skelding	0
CN Woolley	c Wood b Brown	8	b Brown	18
W East	run out	13	b Brown	1
ST Askham	not out	11	lbw b Skelding	3
W Wells	b Brown	1	not out	39
WA Buswell+	c Sidwell b Skelding	20	c Coe b Geary	0
Extras	(b8 nb1)	9	(b9 lb9 nb2)	20
TOTAL		135		176

FOW 1st: 0,24,38,38,39,54,88,94,100
FOW 2nd: 11,17,19,28,28,49,57,100,176

Bowling 1st: Skelding 8-1-23-2 Geary 24-6-53-2 Brown 22-4-45-5 Lord 2-0-5-0
Wood 1-1-0-0 King 2-2-0-0

Bowling 2nd: Skelding 23-1-55-4 Geary 11.5-2-36-2 Brown 20-3-48-4 Lord 4-1-12-0 Wood 1-0-5-0

LEICESTERSHIRE

CJB Wood*	c Vials b Smith	22		b Wells	0
H Whitehead	b Wells	1		c Buswell b East	1
A Lord	lbw b Thompson	3		b Thompson	12
JH King	b Wells	124		c East b Thompson	24
AT Sharp	c Vials b Smith	2		absent	
S Coe	b Wells	39	(5)	c JS Denton b East	26
JW Middleton	lbw b Wells	0	(6)	c Buswell b Thompson	2
TE Sidwell+	b Wells	10	(7)	b East	0
G Geary	b Wells	0	(8)	not out	8
W Brown	c Thompson b Wells	10	(9)	b Thompson	0
A Skelding	not out	1	(10)	lbw b Thompson	0
Extras	(b6 lb3 w1 nb6)	16		(b5 nb1)	6
TOTAL		228			79

FOW 1st: 5,17,46,54,129,137,163,166,217
FOW 2nd: 0,11,11,25,69,69,75,79,79

Bowling 1st: Wells 24-3-82-7 Thompson 19-6-38-1 East 21-9-34-0 Smith 18-6-38-2
Woolley 3-0-12-0 Askham 4-0-8-0

Bowling 2nd: Wells 3-1-6-1 Thompson 18.4-8-39-5 East 17-8-17-3 Smith 7-4-11-1

NORTHAMPTONSHIRE WON BY 4 RUNS

ESSEX

11, 13, 14 June 1921 at Northampton

In an otherwise depressing summer for Northamptonshire, eighteen-year-old Wilfrid Timms carved himself a niche in the club's history with an innings straight out of Sir Henry Newbolt's *Vitaï Lampada*: 'But the voice of a schoolboy rallies the ranks/Play up! Play up! and play the game!'

Timms was 'born into' Northamptonshire cricket. From his family's home in Clarke Road, backing onto the County Ground, he heard the shout that greeted the one-wicket victory over Lancashire in 1908. He scored plenty of runs at Northampton Grammar School, and although his first-class debut against Kent in May 1921 was not a success, a timely century for the Club and Ground side against the Druids persuaded the selection committee to take another look when Essex visited Wantage Road.

Having conceded 616 for five declared in the previous match against Surrey at The Oval, Northamptonshire's weary bowlers were taken to the cleaners again, this time by Jack Freeman with 286 in a touch under seven hours. Despite a dogged 69 from George Thompson – by then a veteran of forty-three and playing principally as a batsman following a serious illness in 1918 – the reply fizzled out for 223. Northamptonshire followed on and ended the day at 63 for one, still needing a further 318 to make Essex bat again.

Determined as you like, Timms – stumped for 23 in the first innings – settled in with the county's player of the season, Bob Haywood. The pair safely negotiated the morning session with the teenager content to play a supporting role, and his half-century, completed just after lunch, was greeted by enthusiastic applause 'out of all proportion to the number of spectators,' according to the *Daily Echo*. The crowd had grown considerably, however, by the time he neared his hundred, boosted by his schoolmates who made the short walk up Ardington Road to see how 'Wilf' was getting on. Moments before tea, Timms pushed a single past square leg to reach three figures after four-and-a-quarter hours in the middle. When the captains called a halt at 6 o'clock, he was still there on 154.

His friends chaired him from the field, and were even more delighted when the school governors declared an extra day's holiday in honour of Timms' great achievement. The messages of congratulations poured in, and the retired teacher of modern languages still had them all – preserved in an old examination register – at the time of his death in 1986. 'It was a good show and I am glad because I know you won't have any more bounce than if you made 10' wrote his proud brother, Bert. 'Has anyone like Lilford (the fifth Baron Lilford, Northamptonshire's long-serving president) bought you any kit yet?' That particular sponsorship deal may not have materialised, but he did get a new cricket bag from a member of the committee, a bat from 'Pat' Darnell and the match ball from his captain, 'Punch' Raven.

Schoolboy hero Wilfrid Timms trots out to bat at the County Ground, with the tennis courts – now the Ken Turner Indoor School – in the background.

Essex won the toss and elected to bat

Umpires: JH Board & FW Marlow

ESSEX

GG Farnfield	b Thomas	0
CAG Russell	c Ball b Woolley	108
JR Freeman+	b Woolley	286
PA Perrin	c Woolley b Thomas	77
G Carter	c Buswell b Raven	44
JG Dixon	c Murdin b Woolley	49
JP Herringshaw	lbw b Woolley	3
P Toone	not out	4
NH Saint		
LJ Phillips		
AD Martin		
Extras	(b14 lb16 w3)	33
TOTAL	(7 wkts dec.)	604

FOW 1st: 4,193,345,475,552,587,604

Bowling 1st: Murdin 34-6-124-0 Thomas 42-10-125-2 Woolley 37-9-90-4 Haywood 4-0-24-0 Ball 15-3-65-0 Thompson 7-1-27-0 Beers 5-0-38-0 Timms 12-0-63-0 Raven 5-0-15-1

NORTHAMPTONSHIRE

RO Raven*	c Farnfield b Toone	24			
CN Woolley	lbw b Dixon	15		b Russell	50
RA Haywood	c Herringshaw b Dixon	13		c Farnfield b Dixon	132
WW Timms	st Freeman b Martin	23		not out	154
GJ Thompson	b Toone	69		st Freeman b Herringshaw	58
EF Tomkins	c Herringshaw b Martin	0			
HG Beers	b Martin	4	(6)	run out	10
KJ Ball	b Dixon	49	(1)	b Martin	8
WA Buswell+	b Toone	7			
JV Murdin	lbw b Toone	0			
AE Thomas	not out	0			
Extras	(b12 lb5 w1 nb1)	19		(b16 lb12 w5)	33
TOTAL		223		(5 wkts)	445

FOW 1st: 25,47,68,98,98,104,205,223,223
FOW 2nd: 25,237,294,417,445

Bowling 1st: Dixon 19.3-3-53-3 Toone 22-1-96-4 Herringshaw 8-5-12-0 Martin 11-0-43-3

Bowling 2nd: Dixon 29-5-88-1 Toone 28-4-85-0 Herringshaw 16-2-63-1 Martin 21-1-81-1 Russell 23-10-28-1 Saint 12-1-37-0 Perrin 1-0-6-0 Carter 4-0-18-0 Phillips 0.2-0-6-0

MATCH DRAWN

WORCESTERSHIRE
11, 13, 14 July 1925 at Kidderminster

Chester Road, Kidderminster has been a happy hunting ground for Northamptonshire's batsmen down the years. In 1946, Dennis Brookes stroked 200 and shared an opening partnership of 243 with Percy Davis. Half a century later, David Sales set all manner of records by hitting an unbeaten 210 on his first-class debut at the age of eighteen. But even more remarkable, arguably, was the county's one-wicket victory on their first visit there, in 1925.

In terms of Championship wins, it was Northamptonshire's most successful inter-war season, and much of the credit belonged to the new captain. Maurice Fitzroy played at the County Ground in 1924 for the Pytchley Hunt against the Grafton, and was a cheerful rather than a richly-talented cricketer. But he could hit and catch a ball, and proved a popular leader who didn't miss a Championship match all summer. Northamptonshire were also helped that year by 100 wickets from P.A. 'Bill' Wright, a former Cambridge blue. This was to be his only full season of county cricket, but he and Vallance Jupp – who performed the first of his eight 'doubles' for Northamptonshire after joining from Sussex as player/secretary in 1922 – were the individual stars in a happy side.

The fast bowling of Wright and 'Nobby' Clark, and a valuable knock from 'Dick' Woolley, put Northamptonshire 21 runs ahead on first innings, only for Maurice Foster to tilt the balance back in Worcestershire's favour with a forthright 150, including 22 fours. The visitors needed 301 to win, and by the close had lost the wickets of Woolley, R.L. 'Dick' Wright and nightwatchman Ben Bellamy in reducing the target by 60. Next morning, Fred Root bowled 'Fanny' Walden and Jupp with successive balls to leave Northamptonshire reeling at 92 for five.

Jack Timms then joined his unrelated namesake, Wilfrid, in the decisive partnership. The former, another product of Wellingborough School and only eighteen at the time, survived a run-out scare with his score in the thirties, and the pair added 140 for the sixth wicket until Jack perished in Root's leg trap just after lunch with 69 runs still needed. Fitzroy wielded the long handle to useful effect, hitting 27 of the next 40 before Root removed him, but 'Bill' Wright went for a duck and then, horror of horrors, Wilfrid Timms departed for a sterling 114. Enter Clark to join Vernon 'Merry' Murdin at 296 for nine – five runs from victory.

Clark accepted batting, according to R.C. Robertson-Glasgow, as 'a professional duty', while Murdin passed 50 only once in 278 first-class innings. Fitzroy, naval officer and gentleman that he was, couldn't bear to watch and shut himself in the gents. But there was no cause for alarm; the last pair squeezed and squirted the necessary runs, and Northamptonshire edged home at the end of a magnificent afternoon's cricket. It was all, as *Wisden* noted, 'most unexpected.'

Northamptonshire's victorious team at Kidderminster in 1925. From left to right, standing: F.I. Walden, L. Bullimer (scorer), J.V. Murdin, E.W. Clark, C.N. Woolley, B.W. Bellamy, J.E. Timms. Seated: R.L. Wright, P.A. Wright, J.M. Fitzroy (captain), V.W.C. Jupp, W.W. Timms.

Worcestershire won the toss and elected to bat

Umpires: T Flowers & TM Russell

WORCESTERSHIRE

FA Pearson	b Murdin	32		b Clark	8
AW Robinson	b Clark	2 (3)		b PA Wright	9
CV Tarbox	b Clark	2 (2)		b Clark	1
GEB Abell+	b Jupp	39		run out	32
CF Root	lbw b PA Wright	28		c RL Wright b Clark	1
MK Foster*	c JE Timms b PA Wright	23		c Woolley b PA Wright	150
WM Hampton	c JE Timms b PA Wright	5		b Jupp	4
JB Coventry	c PA Wright b Clark	12		b Clark	37
HO Rogers	not out	0		not out	50
GC Wilson	c&b Clark	1		b Clark	8
GC Harris	b PA Wright	1		lbw b Clark	0
Extras	(lb4)	4		(b10 lb10 w1)	21
TOTAL		149			321

FOW 1st: 7,17,75,89,120,133,144,144,145
FOW 2nd: 4,19,19,44,83,104,199,300,315

Bowling 1st: Clark 15-2-30-4 PA Wright 21.2-5-58-4 Murdin 8-1-13-1 Jupp 15-4-44-1

Bowling 2nd: Clark 25.4-3-77-6 PA Wright 22-2-116-2 Murdin 7-1-23-0 Jupp 14-0-72-1 Woolley 4-2-12-0

NORTHAMPTONSHIRE

CN Woolley	c Abell b Rogers	45		c Coventry b Root	9
WW Timms	b Root	0		c Coventry b Root	114
JM Fitzroy*	b Pearson	24 (8)		c Wilson b Root	27
RL Wright	lbw b Root	2		b Pearson	0
VWC Jupp	c Hampton b Root	21 (6)		b Root	0
JE Timms	lbw b Root	4 (7)		c Coventry b Root	72
FI Walden	c Robinson b Root	11 (5)		b Root	29
BW Bellamy+	b Root	19 (3)		b Root	14
PA Wright	lbw b Rogers	6		b Pearson	0
JV Murdin	not out	11		not out	9
EW Clark	lbw b Rogers	2		not out	5
Extras	(b13 lb12)	25		(b10 lb13)	23
TOTAL		170		(9 wkts)	302

FOW 1st: 1,33,44,114,118,124,131,137,165
FOW 2nd: 28,48,51,92,92,232,278,280,296

Bowling 1st: Root 29-13-50-6 Pearson 15-6-27-1 Rogers 16.4-1-58-3 Tarbox 2-0-10-0

Bowling 2nd: Root 51-11-124-7 Pearson 43-12-81-2 Rogers 11-3-30-0 Tarbox 3-0-14-0 Wilson 6-1-20-0 Harris 2-0-10-0

NORTHAMPTONSHIRE WON BY 1 WICKET

KENT

19, 20 June 1929 at Northampton

Edward Winchester Clark and Alfred Harry Bakewell – alias 'Nobby' and 'Fred' – brought an unmistakable touch of class to the Northamptonshire side during the grimmest period in the county's first-class history. Clark, the left-arm fast bowler with an action so immaculate it was used in an advertisement for Worthington's beer, and Bakewell, the boy from approved school who became one of the club's all-time batting greats, were both seen to good effect in this two-day trouncing of Kent, achieved with an all-professional team.

The regular captain, Vallance Jupp, was ruled out with a reported combination of food poisoning and a sore foot after treading on a nail in his garage. No other amateurs were available, so the leadership passed to the senior pro, 'Dick' Woolley. The elder brother of the great Frank, he was a rock-solid presence at the top of the Northamptonshire order for twenty years until 1931 when, at the age of forty-five, he was released in the wake of the club's latest financial crisis. On this Wednesday morning, he threw the new ball to Clark, who proceeded to hit the stumps six times – his victims including Woolley junior – to hustle out Kent for 118.

Bakewell had made his Northamptonshire debut the previous summer, and immediately delighted Jupp with his prowess as a short-leg fielder. Five of the eight catches he held in the match against Essex at Leyton, still a club record, were off his captain's bowling. As a batsman, he was identified from a very early stage as a 'natural.' His two-eyed stance didn't delight the purists, but wise coaches, not least the South African Aubrey Faulkner, knew to leave well alone. After failing to score a century in 1928, he proceeded to rectify that state of affairs against a Kent attack including the prolific 'Tich' Freeman, who finished the '29 season with 267 wickets. Bakewell's 137 was made out of 217 in two-and-three-quarter hours, and his best support came from Jack Timms who helped him add 82 for the third wicket. It was the first of his 29 hundreds for the county, and certainly one of the best.

Northamptonshire being their usual exasperating selves, the last six wickets then fell for 49 and Woolley had to make do with a lead of 148. It was more than enough. Clark, whose maiden Test appearance against South Africa was only two months away, picked up three more wickets, as did Albert 'Taffy' Thomas, while seventeen-year-old Reg Partridge from Wollaston, playing his third Championship match, accounted for Bill Ashdown and Leslie Ames. Ben Bellamy and Arthur Cox went out with one run needed, and a no-ball gave Northamptonshire's professionals both an emphatic victory and an always-welcome day off.

C.N. 'Dick' Woolley – Northamptonshire's acting captain in the comprehensive 1929 home win over Kent.

Kent won the toss and elected to bat

Umpires: D Denton & J Moss

KENT

HTW Hardinge	c Liddell b Matthews	18		c Bellamy b Thomas	10
WH Ashdown	b Clark	0	(5)	b Partridge	1
FE Woolley	b Clark	16		retired hurt	33
LEG Ames+	c Matthews b Thomas	2		c Liddell b Partridge	10
CP Johnstone	b Clark	0	(6)	c Walden b Clark	26
GB Legge*	b Clark	32	(7)	c Thomas b Clark	13
GS Watson	c Bellamy b Clark	2	(2)	b Matthews	29
LJ Todd	b Partridge	19		lbw b Thomas	7
AC Wright	b Clark	14		b Thomas	10
AE Watt	not out	6		b Clark	0
AP Freeman	b Clark	8		not out	5
Extras	(b1)	1		(lb2 nb2)	4
TOTAL		118			148

FOW 1st: 1,27,32,33,55,70,75,103,103
FOW 2nd: 27,42,43,54,77,114,115,135,148

Bowling 1st: Clark 16-4-45-7 Thomas 12-1-28-1 Matthews 7-0-29-1 Partridge 5-1-15-1

Bowling 2nd: Clark 20.4-1-67-3 Thomas 25-9-42-3 Matthews 10-1-23-1 Partridge 5-1-12-2

NORTHAMPTONSHIRE

CN Woolley*	b Wright	8			
AH Bakewell	b Wright	137			
BW Bellamy+	c&b Freeman	16	(1)	not out	0
JE Timms	c Freeman b Hardinge	41			
FI Walden	b Hardinge	5			
AL Cox	lbw b Ashdown	17	(2)	not out	0
AG Liddell	st Ames b Freeman	1			
ADG Matthews	b Freeman	20			
AE Thomas	not out	3			
RJ Partridge	b Freeman	0			
EW Clark	b Freeman	9			
Extras	(b8 lb1)	9		(nb1)	1
TOTAL		266		(0 wkt)	1

FOW 1st: 16,65,147,165,217,233,243,256,256

Bowling 1st: Wright 19-5-48-2 Ashdown 8-1-37-1 Freeman 21.2-5-61-5 Watt 7-0-30-0 Woolley 6-0-42-0 Hardinge 15-5-39-2

NORTHAMPTONSHIRE WON BY 10 WICKETS

The Australians

9, 11, 12 August 1930 at Northampton

He possessed, according to the *Northampton Chronicle and Echo*'s excited reporter, 'the eye of an eagle and wrists of steel.' He had already scored double-centuries against two county attacks, Worcestershire and Surrey, and had plundered England's bowlers for 254 at Lord's and 334 – including 309 in a day – at Headingley. Now, the twenty-one-year-old Donald Bradman was to pit his skills against Northamptonshire at Wantage Road.

The Australians drove into town from Birmingham in their fleet of shiny Armstrong-Siddeley motor cars, settled into their rooms at the Grand Hotel (the proprietor was 'Punch' Raven, who had captained Northamptonshire to defeat by an innings and 484 runs against Warwick Armstrong's side in 1921) and enjoyed a Friday night performance of *Abie's Irish Rose* at the New Theatre. Then it was down to business. The Ashes series stood all-square at one victory apiece, and the deciding Test at The Oval – to be played to a finish – would begin in a week's time. Three days against the County Championship's bottom team was unlikely to provide the ideal preparation for Bill Woodfull's men.

Around 9,000 spectators filled the ground on the Saturday morning and witnessed the early demise of the old guard in the shape of 'Dick' Woolley and Rawlins Hawtin – aged forty-four and forty-seven respectively. Northamptonshire's revival was led by two representatives of the rising generation, Fred Bakewell and Jack Timms, just twenty-one and twenty-three. They posted 115 for the third wicket and at least ensured respectability, but Bradman and company returned on Monday, refreshed by a spot of Sunday afternoon tennis at Loddington Hall (home of the club's president, Stephen Schilizzi) and looking forward to their pre-Test batting practice.

Rain delayed the start until 12.15 p.m., and the Australians made sluggish progress against the county's Welsh-born new ball pair, Albert Thomas and Austin Matthews. Thomas sent back Archie Jackson early, bringing in Bradman, and he was unbeaten on 20 at lunch. Then, as the pitch dried out, Thomas and Vallance Jupp – pushing forty but still an off-spinner of great skill and cunning – began to warm to their task. Jupp forced Bradman to play on, and also picked off Woodfull and Alan

Northamptonshire v. *the Australians, 1930. From left to right, back row: A.L. Cox, A.H. Bakewell, J.E. Timms. Middle row: A.G. Liddell, E.L. a'Beckett, A. Hurwood, A.E. Thomas, A.D.G. Thomas, A.F. Kippax, C.N. Woolley, A.A. Jackson, V.Y. Richardson. Front row: T.W. Wall, C.W. Walker, D.G. Bradman, E.F. Towell, W.M. Woodfull, Stephen Schilizzi (Northamptonshire president), V.W.C. Jupp, A.G. Fairfax, A.P.R. Hawkin, P.M. Hornibrook, B.W. Bellamy.*

Fairfax; Thomas breached Alan Kippax's defences to leave the tourists 65 for five; and Jupp mopped up the tail, leaving the Australians 93 all out – the lowest score of their 31-match programme.

It is not difficult to imagine Jupp's delight as he 'invited' Woodfull to follow on. In the event, there was not much to smile about after that, as the captain himself and Vic Richardson hit centuries to save the match with ease. But there was still time for Bradman to fall again, holing out at square leg off Arthur Cox's leg spin, while Thomas received £2 from the Mayor of Northampton's own wallet in honour of his fine bowling in the first innings. As an amateur, Jupp had to content himself with a glass of something refreshing and the feeling of satisfaction at a job well done.

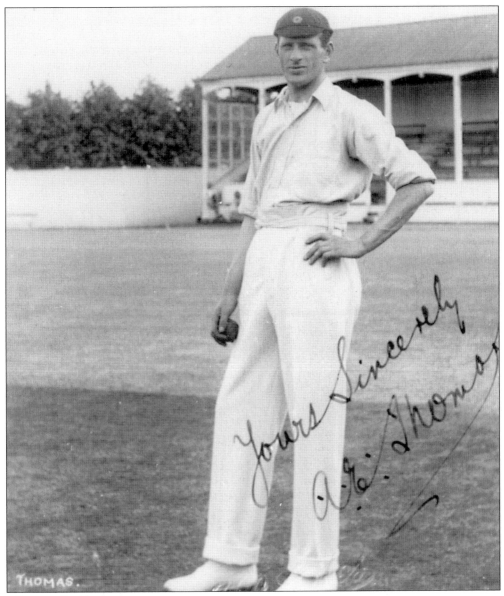

Albert 'Taffy' Thomas.

Bill Woodful in trouble against Northamptonshire in 1930, watched by wicketkeeper Ben Bellamy. Woodfull's men were forced to follow on, but saved the match with ease.

Northamptonshire won the toss and elected to bat

Umpires: F Chester & WR Parry

NORTHAMPTONSHIRE

CN Woolley	b a'Beckett		12
AH Bakewell	c Jackson b Hurwood		84
APR Hawtin	c Wall b Hornibrook		2
JE Timms	c Richardson b Wall		78
VWC Jupp*	c Walker b Hurwood		15
AG Liddell	b Hornibrook		4
AL Cox	b Wall		10
ADG Matthews	hit wkt b Hornibrook		19
BW Bellamy+	not out		10
EF Towell	b Hornibrook		2
AE Thomas	run out		0
Extras	(b3 lb9 nb1)		13
TOTAL			249

FOW 1st: 28,31,146,166,181,208,213,247,249

Bowling 1st: Wall 18-2-53-2 Fairfax 16-5-30-0 a'Beckett 20-9-29-1 Hornibrook 26-11-45-4 Bradman 8-2-31-0 Hurwood 24-8-48-2

AUSTRALIANS

WM Woodfull*	b Jupp	15		c Bellamy b Towell		116
AA Jackson	c&b Thomas	9		c&b Cox		52
DG Bradman	b Jupp	22	(4)	c Hawtin b Cox		35
AG Fairfax	b Jupp	1	(7)	c Bellamy b Timms		1
AF Kippax	b Thomas	10		c Cox b Jupp		20
VY Richardson	c Bellamy b Thomas	7		c Jupp b Towell		116
EL a'Beckett	c Bakewell b Matthews	13	(8)	c&b Matthews		22
A Hurwood	st Bellamy b Jupp	2	(3)	b Jupp		12
PM Hornibrook	b Jupp	2		not out		16
TW Wall	lbw b Jupp	3				
CW Walker+	not out	0				
Extras	(b7 lb2)	9		(b10 lb2 w1 nb2)		15
TOTAL		93		(8 wkts)		405

FOW 1st: 15,51,52,59,65,79,84,84,88
FOW 2nd: 91,106,173,211,300,314,385,405

Bowling 1st: Thomas 29-14-29-3 Matthews 10-3-18-1 Jupp 23.4-10-32-6 Towell 3-0-5-0

Bowling 2nd: Thomas 25-12-32-0 Matthews 35.5-5-83-1 Jupp 21-5-47-2 Towell 24-4-84-2 Cox 28-2-87-2 Liddell 12-3-36-0 Timms 5-1-21-1

MATCH DRAWN

The West Indians

6, 8, 9 May 1933 at Northampton

Mindful, in all probability, of the positive financial implications of putting up a decent show in them, tourist matches seemed to bring out the best in Northamptonshire during the 1930s. Three years after giving Woodfull's Australians a decidedly uncomfortable afternoon, the county welcomed Jackie Grant's West Indians to the first-class section of their English tour by administering a sound thrashing.

Vallance Jupp had lost the captaincy in less-than-amicable circumstances at the end of 1931, to be succeeded by the more diplomatic, less confrontational W.C. 'Beau' Brown. Jupp remained in the side, however, and was to play a significant role in this heartening early-season triumph. He looked likely to make an appearance earlier than anticipated, as Fred Bakewell fell leg-before to 'Manny' Martindale's first ball of the match, swiftly followed by Alex Snowden, the stocky left-hander from Peterborough, and Ben Bellamy. The collapse was halted by Jack Timms and Arthur Cox, who added 121 either side of lunch. Although rapid scoring was out of the question on a slow, damp pitch, Northamptonshire still achieved a serviceable total, with Jupp and Yorkshireman Norman Grimshaw contributing usefully in the middle order.

The attention then centred on George Headley, whose newspaper nickname 'The Black Bradman' was dutifully, if unimaginatively trotted out in the *Chronicle and Echo's* evening headline. While wickets tumbled at the other end to Jupp and 'Nobby' Clark, Headley battled his way to a half-century until the left-armer captured his wicket with the second ball of a new spell, sixth man out at 102. Contemporaries recall that Clark – a moody individual who was sacked twice by Northamptonshire, in 1930 and 1937 – was usually 'in the mood' when he paused to pick the mud out of his spikes at the end of his run. Eager to stake a fresh claim for Test honours in the acrimonious wake of the 'Bodyline' series, he was unquestionably interested in proceedings on that Monday afternoon and followed up his five-wicket haul in the first innings by removing openers Clifford Roach and Edward Hoad when the tourists followed on 159 adrift. Once again, everything depended on Headley. On a showery final

morning, he thumped Jupp for one rasping four, but then misjudged the line against the veteran spinner and was bowled round his legs. After that, the West Indians had little stomach for the fight. Clark returned outstanding match figures of 10-61 from 32 overs and Northamptonshire completed their victory with a minimum of fuss.

By the end of that season, Bakewell had atoned for his 'golden duck' many times over. He made 246 and 257 in successive matches, against Nottinghamshire and Glamorgan, and celebrated his England recall at The Oval in August with 107, against an attack including his County Ground nemesis, Martindale. Aged only twenty-four, he should have had a long and productive career ahead of him. It was not to be. A tragic car accident on 26 August 1936, in which his team-mate Reggie Northway died, ended his first-class cricket career at twenty-seven.

W.C. 'Beau' Brown, a popular skipper who gained a notable victory over the touring West Indians, George Headley and all, in 1933.

Northamptonshire won the toss and elected to bat

Umpires: A Skelding & AE Street

NORTHAMPTONSHIRE

AH Bakewell	lbw b Martindale	0
AW Snowden	b Griffith	5
BW Bellamy+	b da Costa	16
JE Timms	b Merry	64
AL Cox	b Martindale	61
VWC Jupp	c Barrow b Griffith	33
N Grimshaw	st Barrow b Achong	54
WC Brown*	b Headley	18
ADG Matthews	lbw b Martindale	11
AE Thomas	st Barrow b Achong	0
EW Clark	not out	4
Extras	(b15 lb7)	22
TOTAL		288

FOW 1st: 0,16,32,153,158,204,269,276,276

Bowling 1st: Martindale 30.4-5-72-3 Griffith 20-5-48-2 da Costa 26-5-45-1
Achong 53-21-77-2 Merry 9-3-15-1 Headley 3-1-9-1

WEST INDIANS

CA Roach	lbw b Jupp	32		c Bakewell b Clark	0
ELG Hoad	b Clark	2		b Clark	1
GA Headley	lbw b Clark	52	(5)	b Jupp	5
WS Wilde	c Bakewell b Jupp	7	(6)	not out	26
OC da Costa	b Jupp	2	(7)	c Bellamy b Jupp	21
GC Grant*	c Bellamy b Clark	7	(4)	b Clark	20
CA Merry	lbw b Clark	0	(8)	b Matthews	9
I Barrow+	b Matthews	15	(3)	c sub b Thomas	7
EA Martindale	run out	2		c Matthews b Clark	4
HC Griffith	c Bellamy b Clark	0		b Clark	2
EE Achong	not out	1		b Thomas	0
Extras	(b6 lb3)	9		(b1 lb1)	2
TOTAL		129			97

FOW 1st: 5,57,73,79,107,107,108,112,112
FOW 2nd: 2,3,25,29,35,74,87,94,96

Bowling 1st: Clark 15-6-32-5 Thomas 10-5-9-0 Matthews 12.5-4-29-1 Jupp 15-4-30-3 Cox 12-3-20-0

Bowling 2nd: Clark 17-4-29-5 Thomas 17-10-14-2 Matthews 9-5-4-1 Jupp 15-1-48-2

NORTHAMPTONSHIRE WON BY AN INNINGS AND 62 RUNS

Somerset

11, 13, 14 May 1935 at Taunton

At Northamptonshire's Annual General Meeting in March 1935, committee chairman W.C.C. Cooke declared himself confident 'that the club will do a great deal better this year.' A few weeks later the captain, 'Beau' Brown, trod on a ball in the nets and managed only one match all summer. And instead of preparing for another cricket season, Vallance Jupp was serving a prison sentence for manslaughter after his car struck and killed a motorcyclist in January. The omens for the forthcoming campaign were not, in fact, all that propitious.

In Brown's absence, Alex Snowden took charge for the opening Championship game of the season, at Taunton. He and Fred Bakewell carried the score to 65 for one before a familiar collapse saw the situation deteriorate rapidly to 98 for five. Dennis Brookes – a highly promising nineteen-year-old from Yorkshire who made his debut the previous season and was still a fixture at the County Ground more than sixty years later – helped Arthur Cox steady the innings with a 57-run stand for the sixth wicket, but Jack Lee mopped up the lower order and Somerset were only 83 behind at the close of the first day's play with just one man out.

'Nobby' Clark and Reg Partridge bowled Northamptonshire back into the match next morning, reducing the home side to 148 for six, only for 'Box' Case, Arthur Wellard and the tail-enders to secure a lead of 114. The county then needed a good start to their second innings and didn't get it, losing Bakewell, Snowden and Norman Grimshaw with only 20 on the board. Cox was also dismissed before the arrears were cleared, and it was left to nightwatchman Partridge to see out the day with Jack Timms. In fact, Partridge managed to hang around while 50 were added, and Timms went on to a chanceless 131 featuring 19 boundaries. He frequently took a portable gramophone with him on away trips; it would be interesting to know which of his precious 78s inspired him on this occasion.

It was a gutsy effort from Timms, but the match was surely still Somerset's. A victory target of 124 was not expected to pose too many problems, and the Lee brothers scored 14 of them before the first wicket fell. Two runs later, another went down. Soon it was 45 for five, with Clark relishing a strong wind at his back and Austin Matthews proving the perfect foil to his fiery partner. By the time Bill Andrews came in, at 62 for eight, Northamptonshire were nearly home-and-dry. Many years later, Andrews recalled in his autobiography the vicious ball he received from Clark, who 'ran through the crease', apparently still riled by a remark made to him by that ripest of Somerset characters at Kettering three seasons before. Like the elephant, 'Nobby' never forgot.

So the gloom of April gave way to renewed optimism in May. Surely, other wins would follow. And so they did. Eventually.

Austin Matthews – a vital cog in Northamptonshire's attack before his departure to Glamorgan in 1937.

Northamptonshire won the toss and elected to bat

Umpires: JW Hitch & WR Parry

NORTHAMPTONSHIRE

AH Bakewell	c Wellard b Andrews	35		c Hazell b Andrews	0
N Grimshaw	b Wellard	0		c Andrews b Wellard	11
AW Snowden*	lbw b White	29		c Hazell b Andrews	3
JE Timms	b Andrews	2		c JW Lee b Wellard	131
AL Cox	c Burrough b JW Lee	52		lbw b White	39
RJ Partridge	b JW Lee	11		lbw b Andrews	11
D Brookes	c Hazell b JW Lee	20		lbw b Wellard	0
BW Bellamy+	b Hazell	1		c JW Lee b Andrews	1
ADG Matthews	c Wellard b JW Lee	7		b Wellard	35
L Cullen	b JW Lee	0		c Luckes b Wellard	0
EW Clark	not out	4		not out	0
Extras	(b2 lb5 w1 nb2)	10		(b1 lb4 nb1)	6
TOTAL		171			237

FOW 1st: 20,65,69,79,98,155,156,164,164
FOW 2nd: 0,14,20,94,144,145,164,228,228

Bowling 1st: Wellard 17-3-48-1 Andrews 16-2-45-2 JW Lee 11.4-3-31-5 White 20-13-16-1 Hazell 4-0-21-1

Bowling 2nd: Wellard 26.4-8-64-5 Andrews 28-11-54-4 JW Lee 16-2-57-0 White 17-5-44-1 Hazell 9-1-12-0

SOMERSET

JW Lee	c Bellamy b Partridge	59		lbw b Matthews	4
FS Lee	c Partridge b Cox	33		b Clark	9
WT Luckes+	b Clark	4	(9)	lbw b Matthews	13
RA Ingle*	c Cox b Clark	6		b Matthews	4
LC Hawkins	c Clark b Partridge	12	(3)	b Matthews	6
CCC Case	c Bellamy b Partridge	60	(5)	b Clark	11
HD Burrough	c Bellamy b Clark	0	(6)	c Timms b Clark	14
AW Wellard	c Clark b Matthews	38	(7)	b Matthews	2
JC White	not out	23	(8)	lbw b Clark	2
WHR Andrews	c Cullen b Cox	29		lbw b Clark	0
HL Hazell	b Clark	13		not out	4
Extras	(lb3 nb5)	8		(b1 lb3 nb2)	6
TOTAL		285			75

FOW 1st: 80,92,102,108,147,148,218,223,266
FOW 2nd: 14,16,23,31,45,54,56,62,63

Bowling 1st: Clark 30.2-9-63-4 Matthews 30-8-59-1 Partridge 34-4-105-3 Cullen 1-1-0-0 Cox 15-4-50-2

Bowling 2nd: Clark 21-5-38-5 Matthews 20.4-7-31-5

NORTHAMPTONSHIRE WON BY 48 RUNS

LEICESTERSHIRE
27, 29 May 1939 at Northampton

Dennis Brookes was walking into the County Ground on Whit Saturday 1939 and came across a fellow Yorkshireman, the Leicestershire batsman Frank Prentice. 'You know we've got Jack Walsh in the side? It'll be over in two days,' said the super-confident Prentice. It was to prove a remarkably accurate prediction, with just one significant error – Northamptonshire, not Leicestershire, triumphed with a day to spare, giving the county their first Championship win since that blustery afternoon at Taunton in May 1935. It prompted one of cricket journalism's more understated headlines, in the *Chronicle and Echo*: 'Northants Break A Bad Spell.'

The 'spell' in question had extended to 99 County Championship matches, and not surprisingly the team had undergone a substantial transformation in that period; only Dennis Brookes, Jack Timms and Reg Partridge played in the games that began and ended the drought. 'Nobby' Clark, Fred Bakewell, Vallance Jupp and Ben Bellamy had all gone (although Clark was to return after the war) and Austin Matthews joined Glamorgan in 1937. But there was a new captain in Robert Nelson, a Cambridge blue with a few appearances for Middlesex to his credit, who had moved to Northamptonshire to take up a teaching post. He was to prove, in the course of his brief career with the county, a leader worthy of the name.

Leicestershire obligingly brought with them their own loudspeaker van so that gramophone records could be played to entertain the punters during intervals, but the visiting players were emphatically not in a musical mood at lunchtime; Leicestershire were 97 for seven, having been 8 for five after 35 minutes' play, courtesy of Partridge and his new ball partner, Jack Buswell. They rallied slightly to 134 all out, but by Saturday's close Northamptonshire were 280 for two – Brookes 120 not out, Timms on 50 – and already in a commanding position. There had been occasional near-misses during those four bleak years but this time, surely, nothing short of a monsoon could prevent the county finishing the job.

To Nelson's relief, the weather on the Monday did not lend substance to the old music-hall gags about wet Bank Holidays. Around 5,000 spectators filed into the ground, hoping against hope. Brookes' magnificent effort, lasting four-and-a-half hours and including 24 fours, ended just before lunch, but the declaration came at 3.20 p.m., with Northamptonshire's lead worth 376. Maurice Fitzroy, who engendered the team's short-lived revival in 1925, was in the crowd to see New Zealander Bill Merritt make deep inroads with his leg-breaks after Buswell had bowled Les Berry in the first over of Leicestershire's second innings – with a no-ball.

From 53 without loss at tea, the wickets went down in a heap. Merritt's fellow Kiwi, Ken James, was on song behind the stumps with a catch and three stumpings, and ten minutes into the extra half-hour – at twenty-to-seven on May 29 1939 – Northamptonshire rediscovered the seemingly lost art of winning County

Robert Nelson – a gallant Northamptonshire captain, killed in action in 1940.

Championship cricket matches. Supporters swept across the ground, with head groundsman Ron Johnson just managing to save the stumps from the clutches of would-be souvenir hunters.

A speech was demanded, and Nelson obliged: 'I want to pay tribute to the team who have struggled through a trying period without losing heart, and who have kept cheerful in all circumstances. I feel we have welded ourselves into a good side, and I do not think this should be our last victory.' Sadly, Northamptonshire's next Championship success was a world war away, in July 1946. Brookes, Timms, Partridge and Percy Davis were there to play their part in it, but Nelson was not. He died in an air raid on the Royal Marines depot at Deal on 29 October 1940, aged twenty-eight. His characteristically matter-of-fact report on the 1939 season – ' ... at least we were able to put into the field a side capable of commanding some degree of respect from most of the other counties' – was published posthumously in the club's 1946 Yearbook.

Bill Merritt, the last-day hero of the county's drought-breaking victory.

Reg Partridge dismissed Don Bradman for 2 in 1938, and claimed vital wickets against Leicestershire the following year.

Leicestershire won the toss and elected to bat

Umpires: D Hendren & E Cooke

LEICESTERSHIRE

LG Berry	b Buswell	3	b Buswell		31
GS Watson	b Partridge	1	st James b Merritt		36
NF Armstrong	b Partridge	1	lbw b Buswell		20
FT Prentice	lbw b Partridge	1	lbw b Buswell		1
CS Dempster**+	b Buswell	0	b Partridge		10
M Tompkin	run out	32	st James b Merritt		13
GO Dawkes	b Timms	16	c James b Merritt		1
G Lester	not out	44	c Greenwood b Merritt		29
JE Walsh	b Buswell	14	c Partridge b Merritt		4
HA Smith	b Nelson	13	st James b Merritt		8
WH Flamson	b Nelson	0	not out		10
Extras	(b6 lb3)	9	(b7 lb10 nb3)		20
TOTAL		134			183

FOW 1st: 2,6,6,6,8,34,71,97,134
FOW 2nd: 60,100,100,103,120,121,136,152,164

Bowling 1st: Buswell 14-2-43-3 Partridge 13-2-38-3 Merritt 6-0-21-0 Timms 5-0-22-1 Nelson 1.6-0-1-2

Bowling 2nd: Buswell 12-2-47-3 Partridge 12-3-45-1 Merritt 10.7-0-56-6 Timms 6-2-15-0 Nelson 1-1-0-0

NORTHAMPTONSHIRE

HW Greenwood	c Smith b Flamson	8
PC Davis	st Dempster b Walsh	84
D Brookes	c Armstrong b Lester	187
JE Timms	c Tompkins b Flamson	55
RP Nelson*	run out	44
FP O'Brien	b Walsh	10
KC James+	not out	42
MEF Dunkley	c Smith b Flamson	12
WE Merritt	lbw b Flamson	7
RJ Partridge	not out	20
JE Buswell		
Extras	(b30 lb11)	41
TOTAL	(8 wkts dec)	510

FOW 1st: 18,194,295,387,418,421,467,477

Bowling 1st: Flamson 27-2-125-4 Smith 31-1-99-0 Walsh 33-1-157-2 Lester 13-0-60-1 Armstrong 3-0-7-0 Prentice 4-0-21-0

NORTHAMPTONSHIRE WON BY AN INNINGS AND 193 RUNS

LEICESTERSHIRE

2, 4, 5 August 1947 at Leicester

In April 1946, with county cricket about to resume after six years of war, the *Northampton Independent* printed a contribution in verse from G.H. Winterbottom of Cosgrove Hall, supporting Northamptonshire's urgent fund-raising efforts: 'If sixpence from us all were given/From all doubts we should be shriven/Four hundred thousand in the county/Look, my friends, hand out the bounty/Turn my sad and anxious story/To a theme of shining glory.' By August 1947, shining glory – like many other commodities in that era of austerity – was in distinctly short supply around Wantage Road.

As in 1939, it was Leicestershire who gave the county faithful something to smile about. Arriving at Grace Road without a Championship win that season, Northamptonshire turned it on against their neighbours – and unearthed a new bowling talent. Ian Davies, the former sports editor of BBC World Service and a lifelong Northamptonshire supporter, has described it as 'the turning of the tide.' There was, he wrote in the club's 2001 Yearbook, 'more hope for Northamptonshire cricket than there had been for decades; a hope that was to materialise after just one more season … '

The game represented another personal triumph for Dennis Brookes – who was to make his only Test appearance for England against the West Indies the following winter – but on this occasion his pre-match preparation, usually so meticulous and unhurried, was less than ideal. Catching a lift to the ground with Reg Partridge, the pair found themselves held up in traffic and arrived only just in time. The captain, Arthur Childs-Clarke, was not pleased. His mood had mellowed somewhat, however, by the time Northamptonshire's first innings closed for 455; Brookes 210 in five-and-a-half hours with 14 boundaries, Eddie Davis – brother of Percy – a maiden century, and a sixth-wicket stand between the pair worth 259 to retrieve the situation from 78 for five. Even the skipper managed a career-best 68 down the order.

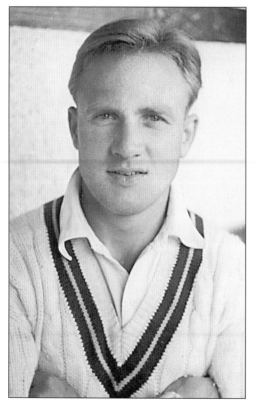

Leicestershire then fell foul of two Clarkes – Bertie, the West Indian leg-spinner and a qualified doctor whose medical duties prevented him accepting the club's offer of the captaincy for 1947, and Bob, the pride of Finedon who was making his debut as a left-arm fast bowler. The latter, with war service on the gruelling arctic convoys behind him, could hardly have launched his first-class career more impressively. In the follow-on, the pace of Jack Webster and slow left-arm of Vince Broderick kept Leicestershire in check, and despite a century from Les Berry the county's target was only 75.

Only? Brookes and Percy Davis went for ducks, Eddie Davis and Broderick followed cheaply, and suddenly there was work to be done. To the rescue came Arthur Cox and Bernard Cornelius, a pillar of local club cricket for whom this was to be the only Championship appearance. He had the pleasure of making the winning hit, earning Northamptonshire their first victory in Leicester since 1927.

Bob Clarke, who had a successful debut against Leicestershire in 1947.

50

Northamptonshire won the toss and elected to bat

Umpires: B Flint & P Holmes

NORTHAMPTONSHIRE

D Brookes	c Watson b Sperry	210		c Lester b Sperry	0
PC Davis	c Walsh b Sperry	14		c Walsh b Jackson	0
BW Cornelius	st Corrall b Walsh	0	(6)	not out	9
AL Cox	c Berry b Lester	2	(3)	not out	41
V Broderick	c Jackson b Walsh	15	(4)	c Corrall b Sperry	5
J Webster	lbw b Walsh	1			
E Davis	lbw b Riddington	104	(5)	b Sperry	18
AW Childs-Clarke*	st Corrall b Walsh	68			
CB Clarke	b Jackson	4			
K Fiddling+	c Corrall b Walsh	10			
RW Clarke	not out	6			
Extras	(b7 lb14)	21		(lb2)	2
TOTAL		455		(4 wkts)	75

FOW 1st: 30,31,46,72,78,337,385,392,436
FOW 2nd: 1,1,16,61

Bowling 1st: Sperry 30-4-66-2 Riddington 29-7-47-1 Walsh 44.4-5-157-5 Lester 20-2-71-1 Jackson 15-3-40-1 Prentice 4-0-15-0 Hales 10-1-38-0

Bowling 2nd: Sperry 12.4-4-37-3 Walsh 7-0-22-0 Jackson 6-1-14-1

LEICESTERSHIRE

LG Berry*	c CB Clarke b Webster	16	lbw b Cox	102
A Riddington	c&b CB Clarke	49	b RW Clarke	5
GS Watson	c&b RW Clarke	22	lbw b Webster	0
M Tompkin	lbw b CB Clarke	47	c Fiddling b Webster	10
VE Jackson	c Cox b RW Clarke	24	b CB Clarke	17
FT Prentice	c Cox b RW Clarke	23	c RW Clarke b Webster	67
G Lester	b RW Clarke	9	b Broderick	40
LA Hales	b CB Clarke	3	lbw b Broderick	11
JE Walsh	c C-Clarke b CB Clarke	15	c Cornelius b CB Clarke	21
P Corrall+	c RW Clarke b CB Clarke	2	b Broderick	21
J Sperry	not out	0	not out	8
Extras	(b5 lb8 nb1)	14	(b1 lb2)	3
TOTAL		224		305

FOW 1st: 31,54,136,145,171,195,206,208,217
FOW 2nd: 5,6,16,60,174,238,252,259,293

Bowling 1st: RW Clarke 27-9-56-4 Webster 18-5-51-1 Broderick 7-0-18-0 CB Clarke 21.4-2-69-5 Cox 6-1-16-0

Bowling 2nd: RW Clarke 30-7-102-1 Webster 17-5-35-3 Broderick 21.2-8-34-3 CB Clarke 28-7-89-2 Cox 7-1-31-1 Childs-Clarke 7-3-11-0

NORTHAMPTONSHIRE WON BY 6 WICKETS

SOMERSET

4, 5, 6 May 1949 at Taunton

It is arguable that the build-up to Northamptonshire's opening County Championship outing of 1949 was at least as dramatic as the match itself. It all begin with the appointment of Freddie Brown, the notable pre-war all-rounder for Surrey and England, as captain in place of Arthur Childs-Clarke – a move made possible by a job offer from the Northampton-based roller bearings manufacturer, British Timken. Brown was thirty-eight, a former POW and a strong, forthright character with opinions to match. Somerset may have been first on the fixture card, but his own initial tussle was to be with Northamptonshire's selection committee.

The story has passed into Wantage Road folklore. Brown walked into the meeting at which the composition of the side for Taunton was being discussed, pulled out a piece of paper and said: 'I'm sorry. I'm the only one, with Dennis Brookes (then senior professional) and Jack Mercer (the club's coach), who has attended all the net practices, and this is the team I want.' He got his way. As the committee minutes recorded: 'The selection of this side has not been unanimously approved by [this] committee, but the captain's view has been accepted.' As Brown observed wryly many years later, it was a good job he won the game.

It was, like Waterloo, a damned close-run thing. The new skipper immediately stamped his authority and personality on proceedings. He demanded of Percy Davis, Brookes' regular opening partner, what he thought he was doing putting his pads on, and went in first himself. Arthur Wellard soon had Brown caught behind, but just about everyone else made runs – a century in Vince Broderick's case, featuring some fluent driving – except for poor Davis who, down at number six, fell to Maurice Tremlett without scoring. For the popular little batsman from Brackley, the writing was on the wall. Fortunately, he would carve out a successful second career as a coach, with Northamptonshire and, later, Harrow School.

There was no obvious deterioration in the pitch on the second day, but no one played a really substantial innings for Somerset as the county's bowlers picked up wickets at regular intervals. Off-spinner Gordon Garlick – like Norman Oldfield and Bert Nutter, a recently-recruited Lancastrian

The 'New Look' Northamptonshire side in 1949. From left to right, back row: F. Jakeman, R.W. Clarke, E. Davis, R.G. Garlick, N. Oldfield, W. Barron, K. Fiddling, P.C. Davis. Front row: V. Broderick, J.E. Timms, F.R. Brown (captain), D. Brookes, A.E. Nutter.

– scythed through the tail, and Brown sent the home side in again needing 186 to avoid losing by an innings. They lost six wickets in wiping out the arrears with the Northamptonshire captain, playing only his second Championship match since 1939 and not surprisingly feeling his back a little, striking four times in the middle order. Immediately after lunch, Brookes and Davis – restored to his accustomed position – went to the crease to knock off the 64 runs required to give Brown the ideal start.

At this point, all the old ghosts returned to haunt the side. As Brown wrote afterwards: 'I really believe that Northamptonshire cricketers were scared at the prospect of winning a match.' Davis went leg-before to Bertie Buse, a decision still debated in the darker recesses of the West Stand. Then Wellard bowled Brookes, and Buse added four more batsmen to his collection to leave the county tottering at 27 for six when Brown came in. Broderick helped him raise the total to 48 before becoming a sixth victim for Buse, who moments later had Bob Clarke stumped. Enter Garlick at 52 for eight with the game still anybody's. But somehow – a push here, a legside swing there – the runs came without further mishap.

It was the first of 'New Look' Northamptonshire's ten Championship victories in 1949, and they finished sixth in the table – dizzy heights not attained since 1913. The visit to Taunton had produced, in Brown's words, 'a very good game of cricket indeed.' It was also, in a wider context, one of the most significant contests in Northamptonshire's chequered history.

Vince Broderick.

Freddie Brown – resplendent in Quidnuncs cap – leads Northamptonshire into the field, 1949.

Northamptonshire won the toss and elected to bat

Umpires: D Hendren & SJ Staples

NORTHAMPTONSHIRE

D Brookes	b Tremlett	32		b Wellard	10
FR Brown*	c Luckes b Wellard	11	(8)	not out	22
N Oldfield	c Luckes b Lawrence	63		b Buse	1
JE Timms	c Gimblett b Tremlett	57		c Lawrence b Buse	4
F Jakeman	c Luckes b Tremlett	48		c Wellard b Buse	8
PC Davis	c Lawrence b Tremlett	0	(2)	lbw b Buse	1
V Broderick	c Woodhouse b Wellard	100	(6)	b Buse	8
AE Nutter	st Luckes b Hazell	41	(7)	b Buse	0
RW Clarke	c M-Innes b Wellard	26		st Luckes b Buse	1
RG Garlick	not out	10		not out	7
K Fiddling+	b Wellard	1			
Extras	(b4 lb4 w3)	11		(lb2)	2
TOTAL		400		(8 wkts)	64

FOW 1st: 18,78,138,210,213,220,310,389,392
FOW 2nd: 2,14,14,24,27,27,48,52

Bowling 1st: Wellard 25.2-6-57-4 Buse 15-2-43-0 Tremlett 32-7-80-4 Hazell 22-7-52-1 Lawrence 35-2-140-1 Gimblett 6-0-17-0

Bowling 2nd: Wellard 10-0-36-1 Buse 9-1-26-7

SOMERSET

H Gimblett	c Nutter b Broderick	51	lbw b Nutter	42
E Hill	lbw b Nutter	4	c Brown b Garlick	37
HTF Buse	c Oldfield b Brown	42	c Clarke b Broderick	9
NS Mitchell-Innes	run out	24	c Fiddling b Garlick	42
M Coope	run out	3	c Timms b Brown	26
GES Woodhouse*	b Brown	5	c Oldfield b Brown	17
MF Tremlett	b Garlick	40	c Clarke b Brown	17
J Lawrence	c Nutter b Garlick	9	c Oldfield b Brown	2
WT Luckes+	not out	9	not out	30
AW Wellard	b Garlick	8	c Garlick b Clarke	14
HL Hazell	c Clarke b Garlick	7	b Clarke	0
Extras	(b10 nb2)	12	(b11 lb1 nb1)	13
TOTAL		214		249

FOW 1st: 17,78,126,130,130,137,179,184,200
FOW 2nd: 60,75,140,147,166,184,200,215,247

Bowling 1st: Clarke 9-3-26-0 Nutter 16-5-33-1 Brown 29-13-60-2 Broderick 26-9-64-1 Garlick 9.3-4-19-4

Bowling 2nd: Clarke 9.4-1-37-2 Nutter 14-2-52-1 Brown 24-12-51-4 Broderick 33-9-50-1 Garlick 18-6-46-2

NORTHAMPTONSHIRE WON BY 2 WICKETS

THE INDIANS
30, 31 July, 1 August 1952 at Northampton

If everyone who claims to have been a spectator at Wantage Road on Wednesday 30 July 1952 really was, then a crowd well in excess of 100,000 must have turned up to watch Dennis Brookes at the top of his form and a twenty-two-year-old tearaway named Frank Tyson make a remarkable first-class debut. The official gate receipts – just over £1,600 for the whole three-day match – would tend to indicate that the attendance was a little lower, but those who really were present certainly had their money's worth.

The 'capture' of Tyson, Lancashire-born and a student at Durham University, represented another feather in the cap of Jock Livingston, the sparky, garrulous left-hander from Sydney later described by Tyson himself as 'the Lord Kitchener of Northamptonshire' for his recruiting prowess. Livingston had faced the young fast bowler in a Sunday afternoon game at Knypersley in Staffordshire and was suitably impressed. Terms were agreed in June 1952 and a few weeks later Freddie Brown, by then an England selector as well as Northamptonshire's captain, picked him in the county's team to face the Indians, who had recently been routed at Old Trafford by Fred Trueman, then twenty-one and playing only his third Test. Might Tyson be a future partner for Trueman at international level?

Most of the journalists in the old 'signal box' led their first-day stories on Brookes' batting. 'Safe, sound and stylish' according to *Wisden*, he hit 16 fours in his 156. Late acceleration came from the club's newest Australian acquisition, George Tribe, and Brown declared to give Tyson a single over before the close. The scribes were soon contemplating a re-write as the newcomer's sheer pace forced stand-in wicketkeeper Brian Reynolds and the slip fielders to 'give it a bit.'

Brown, thoroughly enjoying the spectacle, reckoned it the fastest over he had seen by an English bowler since Harold Larwood on the 'Bodyline' tour two decades earlier. India's opener, Pankaj Roy, was relishing proceedings rather less than Brown, and the sixth ball found the inside edge of his bat. Reynolds, behind the stumps, did the rest. This was just the first faint rustle of a breeze that, within two-and-a-half years, would become English cricket's very own 'Typhoon'.

It was also his only wicket, in a game which petered out to the tamest of draws after rain allowed only two hours' play on the third day. A year later, at the end of his qualification period, Tyson was unleashed against the Australians, and again made headlines with a hostile opening over that accounted for Colin McDonald – leg-before, painfully – and Graeme Hole. Mental notes were made, on both sides of the great Ashes divide.

Frank Tyson.

Northamptonshire won the toss and elected to bat

Umpires: K McCanlis & H Palmer

NORTHAMPTONSHIRE

N Oldfield	c Mantri b Chowdhury	44		run out	45
D Brookes	b Shinde	156		not out	51
L Livingston	c Mantri b Shinde	26			
F Jakeman	c Phadkar b Sarwate	15	(3)	not out	6
DW Barrick	c Chowdhury b Umrigar	30			
MEJC Norman	lbw b Sarwate	17			
FR Brown*	c Gopinath b Sarwate	18			
GE Tribe	not out	38			
BL Reynolds+	not out	12			
RW Clarke					
FH Tyson					
Extras	(b1 lb5 nb3)	9		(b3 w1 nb1)	5
TOTAL	(7 wkts dec)	365		(1 wkt)	107

FOW 1st: 100,172,196,256,290,314,316
FOW 2nd: 91

Bowling 1st: Phadkar 23-8-48-0 Chowdhury 23-2-94-1 Umrigar 8-1-19-1 Shinde 17-2-77-2 Gaekwad 18-2-42-0 Sarwate 18-3-76-3

Bowling 2nd: Phadkar 9-2-28-0 Chowdhury 13-5-21-0 Gaekwad 15-3-33-0 Sarwate 7-0-16-0 Roy 2-0-3-0 Gopinath 1-0-1-0

INDIANS

MK Mantri+	lbw b Clarke	8
PK Roy	c Reynolds b Tyson	0
SG Shinde	c Barrick b Clarke	6
HR Adhikari*	c Tribe b Brown	73
VL Manjrekar	b Barrick	83
PR Umrigar	c Oldfield b Barrick	59
DG Phadkar	not out	29
CD Gopinath	run out	15
CT Sarwate	b Tribe	8
HG Gaekwad	c Oldfield b Brown	1
NR Chowdhury	lbw b Brown	1
Extras	(b19 lb6 nb1)	26
TOTAL		309

FOW 1st: 1,9,39,151,243,256,287,298,299

Bowling: Tyson 21-4-47-1 Clarke 22-8-55-2 Brown 25.2-3-61-3 Tribe 24-0-88-1 Barrick 12-1-32-2

MATCH DRAWN

LANCASHIRE
12, 13, 14 August 1953 at Old Trafford

Going into the Coronation Year fixture up there, Northamptonshire had played 21 County Championship matches at Old Trafford, with 8 defeats, 13 draws and not a single victory. The chances of finally putting something in the 'wins' column this time were not particularly bright; of the twenty players on the staff, only ten were fit. The likes of Jock Livingston, Norman Oldfield, Des Barrick and Bert Nutter were all missing, and then on the morning of the match the captain, Freddie Brown, pulled out as well. Northamptonshire had not taken a twelfth man to Manchester. Who could make up the numbers?

The choice fell on Peter Pickering, a twenty-seven-year-old Yorkshireman better known as a professional footballer; he kept goal for York City, Chelsea, Kettering Town and – later – Northampton Town. Pickering had turned out for the county's Second XI in home and away matches against Cambridgeshire earlier in the season. Working for British Timken, the ultimate sports-friendly employer, he was likely to be released at short notice. And the notice couldn't have been much shorter. The puzzled Pickering was summoned by the works tannoy at 9.15 a.m., given the keys to a car and told to pick up his kit and head for Manchester. In those pre-motorway days, he arrived at lunchtime, and was soon joining his team-mates in the field. Brown drove the Timken car back to Northampton, and then headed on to The Oval where the deciding Test against Australia was to begin in three days' time.

The Old Trafford pitch was a shocker – 'all scratched to bits', according to Dennis Brookes, Northamptonshire's acting-captain. George Tribe's left-arm wrist spin proved too much for the players down the Lancashire order as 133 for five became 163 all out, but despite a handy 22 from Pickering the visitors' reply was an even more dismal affair until the last man, Bob Clarke, came in to join Tribe. Not the most polished of batsmen, nor the most thoughtful, nor the bravest, Clarke managed to stick around in support of the Australian while the points for a first-innings lead were secured. The county finished 14 runs ahead, and with the pitch now 'flying' after rain, only Geoff Edrich – who defied the pain from a bruised hand during his stay of three hours – was able to come to terms with Clarke and Frank Tyson.

But Lancashire had Brian Statham, Roy Tattersall, Malcolm Hilton and Bob Berry, a quartet of England bowlers, and at 40 for five, Northamptonshire's target of 128 looked a long way off. But reputations meant nothing to Pickering, who proceeded to hit 37 out of a 51-run stand with Tribe and cement his place in history – if not in the team for another match. Tribe, with 110 unbeaten runs in the game, renewed his partnership with Clarke, and they chipped and chiselled the last 11 for a famous victory. Less than a week later, The Ashes came home too. Those were heady days indeed.

Peter Pickering (right) with Frank Tyson. He made a mark on proceedings in his only first-class match.

Lancashire won the toss and elected to bat

Umpires: WT Jones & AED Smith

LANCASHIRE

JT Ikin	c Tribe b Lightfoot	25	c Lightfoot b Tyson	0
ND Howard*	b Tyson	3	b Tyson	6
GA Edrich	c Tribe b Clarke	4	not out	81
KJ Grieves	c Reynolds b Clarke	30	c Clarke b Tyson	2
A Wharton	c Davis b Clarke	21	c Tyson b Lightfoot	4
PT Marner	b Tribe	22	b Clarke	5
MJ Hilton	st Reynolds b Broderick	20	c Davis b Clarke	4
FD Parr+	b Tribe	10	c Reynolds b Clarke	10
JB Statham	c Reynolds b Tribe	4	lbw b Clarke	17
R Tattersall	b Tribe	5	c Davis b Clarke	6
R Berry	not out	6	c Tribe b Clarke	0
Extras	(b11 lb2)	13	(b4 lb2)	6
TOTAL		163		141

FOW 1st: 13,30,36,80,95,133,137,147,152
FOW 2nd: 0,11,13,34,49,57,94,125,139

Bowling 1st: Tyson 7-1-14-1 Clarke 15-4-34-3 Lightfoot 7-4-11-1 Tribe 25.2-10-53-4 Broderick 13-3-38-1

Bowling 2nd: Tyson 15-5-30-3 Clarke 21.4-6-60-6 Lightfoot 9-4-27-1 Tribe 5-0-18-0

NORTHAMPTONSHIRE

D Brookes*	c Grieves b Tattersall	0	c Marner b Tattersall	7
V Broderick	b Statham	1	c Parr b Statham	8
E Davis	c Grieves b Tattersall	22	c Wharton b Statham	11
BL Reynolds+	c Edrich b Statham	0	lbw b Statham	8
AP Arnold	c Grieves b Berry	10	lbw b Tattersall	2
GE Tribe	not out	73	not out	37
DG Greasley	c Ikin b Tattersall	10	b Statham	2
PB Pickering	c Berry b Hilton	22	b Hilton	37
A Lightfoot	st Parr b Hilton	1	c Grieves b Berry	3
FH Tyson	b Statham	1	c&b Hilton	0
RW Clarke	b Hilton	20	not out	2
Extras	(b11 lb6)	17	(b4 lb7)	11
TOTAL		177	(9 wkts)	128

FOW 1st: 6,14,15,42,58,71,106,120,125
FOW 2nd: 22,30,37,37,40,91,94,108,117

Bowling 1st: Statham 18-2-54-3 Tattersall 24-8-76-3 Berry 10-2-25-1 Hilton 8-6-5-3

Bowling 2nd: Statham 18-4-44-4 Tattersall 13-2-40-2 Berry 3-0-9-1 Hilton 9-1-24-2

NORTHAMPTONSHIRE WON BY 1 WICKET

ESSEX

With the agitation for 'brighter cricket' as tiresomely persistent as ever, Northamptonshire's chairman 'Tubby' Vials was quick to talk up the fare on offer to county supporters: 'It is difficult to recall a finer example of a cricket match as played by both sides than our game against Essex. No need to write to the papers about the wicket and slow play if all games could be played like that.' Any number of batsmen shone in this entertaining contest, but Jock Livingston proved the brightest star of all.

The setting was perfect. 'The Grove' at Wellingborough School had been used by Northamptonshire as far back as 1884, but not again until 1946. There was talk of staging a 'Cricket Week' there in the 1930s, only for the proposal to fall foul of the headmaster, Lyonulph de Orellana Tollemache, who doubted whether the pitch would be up to it. Any lingering fears on that score were assuaged in 1949 when the county's game against Yorkshire produced 1,085 runs for the loss of only 18 wickets – Len Hutton helping himself to 269 not out.

Superstition demanded, and still demands today, that any batsman wishing to prosper must set foot on W.G. Grace's doorstep, placed in front of the thatched pavilion in 1940 after a 'mercy dash' to Bristol – where the Doctor's old home was being demolished – by Wellingborough's cricket-mad master, Murray Witham. It must have taken a proper pounding on those three days in 1955. Charlie Williams, Oxford captain and future life peer, led the way for Essex, with Trevor Bailey and Doug Insole also contributing half-centuries. The most successful bowler was Northampton-born off-spinner John Wild, whose son Duncan followed him into the side in the 1980s. Raman Subba Row, recruited from Surrey the previous winter, bolstered Northamptonshire's reply, which nevertheless came up 86 short. Ray Smith then smashed a 73-minute century, the fastest of the season, and Insole's declaration left the home team needing 332 in 3 hours and 20 minutes.

It wasn't felt to be an over-generous target in the Northamptonshire dressing room, but Livingston – who came to the crease to replace the injured Dennis Brookes – immediately set about the Essex attack with relish. 'Jock never thought leg-spinners could bowl,' recalls Brian Reynolds, and Bill Greensmith duly disappeared for 65 runs in eight overs. The quick-footed left-hander raced to 82 in just under an hour and put Smith's record in jeopardy, only to ease up a little as he and New Zealander Peter Arnold, who became the club's president in 1996, picked off runs almost at will. Subba Row, Des Barrick and George Tribe all chipped in, but Livingston reigned supreme with 2 sixes and 23 fours in an innings lasting 160 minutes in all. Northamptonshire got there with a quarter-of-an-hour to spare – the fourth in a sequence of six successive victories, a record equalled but never surpassed in the county's history.

The JOCK LIVINGSTON TESTIMONIAL HANDBOOK

Contributors
include
Sir
DONALD BRADMAN
JOHN ARLOTT
and
LEN HUTTON

1/-

A fund-raising brochure for Northamptonshire's outstanding left-hander from Sydney, Jock Livingston.

Essex won the toss and elected to bat

Umpires: TJ Bartley & D Davies

ESSEX

TC Dodds	lbw b Tyson	1		b Tribe		29
G Barker	b Tribe	30		lbw b Tribe		51
TE Bailey	c Subba Row b Wild	72				
CCP Williams	b Wild	93		b Tribe		0
DJ Insole*	lbw b Wild	57		lbw b Broderick		45
PA Gibb+	b Wild	28	(7)	not out		0
R Smith	c Tribe b Broderick	7	(6)	not out		101
R Horsfall	not out	44	(3)	st Andrew b Broderick		17
WT Greensmith	not out	5				
LHR Ralph						
KC Preston						
Extras	(b4 lb8 nb2)	14		(lb2)		2
TOTAL	(7 wkts dec)	351		(5 wkts dec)		245

FOW 1st: 2,45,193,202,261,272,328
FOW 2nd: 62,97,97,101,241

Bowling 1st: Tyson 18-3-57-1 Webster 20-7-37-0 Barrick 6-2-17-0 Tribe 23-6-67-1 Broderick 23-11-46-1 Subba Row 4-0-15-0 Wild 23-4-98-4

Bowling 2nd: Webster 9-0-38-0 Barrick 4-0-10-0 Tribe 27.2-8-80-3 Broderick 20-7-57-2 Subba Row 2-0-19-0 Wild 10-3-39-0

NORTHAMPTONSHIRE

D Brookes*	b Bailey	9	retired hurt		14
AP Arnold	lbw b Preston	18	c Preston b Insole		80
L Livingston	c Horsfall b Ralph	41	not out		172
DW Barrick	c Insole b Ralph	17	b Bailey		22
R Subba Row	not out	90	c&b Insole		14
GE Tribe	st Gibb b Greensmith	31	not out		28
V Broderick	c Williams b Greensmith	10			
KV Andrew+	b Greensmith	1			
J Wild	st Gibb b Smith	25			
J Webster	c Insole b Bailey	3			
FH Tyson	b Preston	5			
Extras	(b4 lb9 nb2)	15	(lb2 w1 nb1)		4
TOTAL		265	(3 wkts)		334

FOW 1st: 22,30,82,99,161,179,187,216,252
FOW 2nd: 183,251,288

Bowling 1st: Bailey 17-3-50-2 Preston 12.5-1-44-2 Ralph 15-3-46-2 Smith 26-10-36-1 Greensmith 21-3-74-3

Bowling 2nd: Bailey 21-3-58-1 Preston 6-0-35-0 Ralph 4-0-34-0 Smith 8-0-63-0 Greensmith 8-0-65-0 Insole 12-0-65-2 Barker 1-0-6-0 Williams 0.1-0-4-0

NORTHAMPTONSHIRE WON BY 7 WICKETS

Surrey

28, 30, 31 May 1957 at The Oval

When Northamptonshire claimed the runners-up spot to Yorkshire in the County Championship of 1912, they had been genuine title contenders for much of the season. This was not the case in 1957, the summer of the club's next second-place finish. Dennis Brookes' team trailed in 94 points behind Surrey, who secured the crown as early as 16 August and thus became champions for the sixth year running. But in the head-to-head contests between the two counties, Northamptonshire had much to be proud of. They beat Surrey at Northampton in 1955, did a home-and-away 'double' over them in 1956, and completed a fourth straight win in this game at The Oval, coinciding with England's opening Test against the West Indies at Edgbaston.

Peter May, Jim Laker and Tony Lock were all absent on international duty, but no team containing the likes of Alec and Eric Bedser, Peter Loader, Ken Barrington and Micky Stewart could be described as weak. They enjoyed much the better of the early exchanges, with Loader finding plenty of life in a well-grassed pitch, and it took a gritty ninth-wicket stand of 36 between George Tribe and Keith Andrew to carry Northamptonshire into three figures. Frank Tyson then responded in kind, reducing Surrey 71 to four at the close and forcing Tom Clark to retire with a crack on the hand.

Next day, Tyson returned the best bowling figures of his first-class career, eclipsing (at least statistically) his match-winning seven for 27 in the New Year Test at Melbourne in 1955. It was a rare treat for Tyson to bowl for Northamptonshire on a strip offering him some help. The club's policy of preparing – or, rather, not preparing – surfaces to suit the spin of Tribe, Jack Manning and Mick Allen did nothing for their England paceman; indeed, Len Hutton advised Tyson to forsake the 'cabbage patch specials' at Wantage Road and return to his native Lancashire if he wanted to extend his time in Test cricket. In fact, he retired from the first-class game in 1960 at the age of thirty.

Surrey scraped the first-innings points on Thursday morning, but Brookes proceeded to make yet another vital contribution in the shape of a four-hour century that completed his 'set' against the other 16 counties. He and Des Barrick added 92 for the third wicket, easily the highest partnership of the game, and when Surrey set about trying to score 230 for victory, they lost Stewart to Tyson without a run on the board at the tail-end of the day. The task subsequently proved beyond them as 'Typhoon' took his match haul to 13 for 112, mopping up with three wickets in nine balls after lunch.

'Runner-up was a good position,' wrote John Arlott at the end of the summer. 'It is no criticism of Northamptonshire's feat to continue to compare them with Surrey, for that comparison went on round the dressing rooms of England all last season.' It was, quite simply, the county's misfortune to be strong at a time when Surrey, day in and day out, were stronger.

Dennis Brookes in action, in a post-war Test Trial.

Northamptonshire won the toss and elected to bat

Umpires: WE Phillipson & J Wood

NORTHAMPTONSHIRE

D Brookes*	c Stewart b AV Bedser	9	c Fletcher b Loader	100
AP Arnold	lbw b Loader	8	c Willett b Loader	26
L Livingston	lbw b Loader	22	c Stewart b AV Bedser	12
DW Barrick	c Cox b Loader	4	c AV Bedser b Barrington	57
BL Reynolds	c Barrington b AV Bedser	7	c&b Barrington	0
GE Tribe	c Constable b Cox	38	c McIntyre b AV Bedser	2
JS Manning	c Barrington b AV Bedser	1	c sub b AV Bedser	11
FH Tyson	c Barrington b AV Bedser	2	b AV Bedser	2
MHJ Allen	b AV Bedser	1	c Cox b Loader	1
KV Andrew+	b EA Bedser	16	c Barrington b AV Bedser	5
HRA Kelleher	not out	0	not out	0
Extras	(lb3 nb2)	5	(b8 lb4 nb4)	16
TOTAL		113		232

FOW 1st: 11,24,38,48,66,67,73,75,111
FOW 2nd: 64,94,186,186,191,219,224,225,228

Bowling 1st: Loader 26-5-51-3 AV Bedser 24-7-28-5 Cox 12.1-2-27-1 EA Bedser 3-1-2-1

Bowling 2nd: Loader 22-2-68-3 AV Bedser 25.5-6-51-5 Cox 11-1-38-0 EA Bedser 11-3-25-0 Barrington 11-1-34-2

SURREY

TH Clark	c Andrew b Tyson	3	lbw b Tribe	10
MJ Stewart	b Manning	24	c Allen b Tyson	0
B Constable	c Allen b Tyson	11	b Manning	29
KF Barrington	b Tyson	4	c Arnold b Tribe	5
DGW Fletcher	c sub b Tyson	29	c Kelleher b Tyson	12
MD Willett	b Tyson	4	c Reynolds b Manning	26
DF Cox	c Tribe b Tyson	5	b Tribe	54
EA Bedser	b Kelleher	17	c Andrew b Tyson	1
AJW McIntyre+	c Andrew b Tyson	7	b Tyson	0
PJ Loader	c&b Tyson	7	b Tyson	4
AV Bedser*	not out	3	not out	12
Extras	(nb2)	2	(b4)	4
TOTAL		116		157

FOW 1st: 20,32,56,63,71,92,102,106,107
FOW 2nd: 0,54,77,102,102,103,103,130,135

Bowling 1st: Tyson 20.5-2-60-8 Kelleher 23-6-46-1 Manning 7-2-8-1

Bowling 2nd: Tyson 22-7-52-5 Kelleher 8-3-19-0 Manning 12.3-9-12-2 Tribe 25-6-64-3 Allen 2-1-6-0

NORTHAMPTONSHIRE WON BY 72 RUNS

YORKSHIRE

2, 3, 4 July 1958 at Northampton

George Tribe turned up at Northamptonshire's Former Players' Reunion in 2001, his first visit in more than a decade, and the spry, blue-blazered octogenarian was almost late for his lunch as county supporters with memories of his glory days gathered round to shake his hand and relive their favourite Tribe moment. It was, he admitted, 'quite embarrassing really,' although any cricketer with 1,021 wickets and seven 'doubles' for Northamptonshire is bound to occupy a special place in the affections of those who care about the club. While accepting the fact that sporting heroes come in all shapes and sizes, it was difficult to imagine this dapper Aussie as a ruthless destroyer of reputations and batting averages. But he was just that – especially if they happened to belong to Yorkshiremen.

In 1908, Northamptonshire had managed only 42 runs in their two innings against George Hirst and Schofield Haigh; half-a-century later, it was Yorkshire's turn to taste humiliation. Tribe had captured 15 for 75 in the match at Bradford in May 1955, only to finish on the losing side by 78 runs. His performance at Wantage Road in 1958 was even more spectacular, and secured the right result. 'Yorkshire had the reputation of not being able to play wrist spin, and in fairness the type of pitches they had up there were more likely to breed finger spinners,' he recalled charitably. This Northampton strip, saturated by the rain that prevented any play on the first day, gave Tribe all the encouragement he needed, and when the game finally got underway on Thursday, only Brian Close – playing what *Wisden* described as 'a model innings' – offered any serious resistance after Raman Subba Row put the visitors in. He scored 46 out of his side's 67 all out; the next-highest score was 7, by Frank Lowson (Tribe's first victim, caught by Micky Allen at short leg) and extras. Before the day was out, cut short by a heavy thunderstorm, Northamptonshire had been dismissed too, by Johnny Wardle and Ray Illingworth, but still led by 40.

It might as well have been 400. Yorkshire's openers trooped out again at a quarter-to two on Friday, and by four o'clock their second effort was over – all out for 65. Tribe was virtually unplayable, utilising his full repertoire of back-of-the-hand variations, and took eight wickets in 24 balls at a personal cost of four runs. His match return, 15 for 31, is one club record unlikely ever to be beaten, certainly as long as pitches remain covered. Even the *County Yearbook*, noted for its bland understatement, declared that Tribe 'bowled magnificently'. With more rain falling, Northamptonshire knocked off the runs necessary to complete a nine-wicket triumph. The torture inflicted by Hirst and Haigh on Tim Manning's team in 1908 had been avenged by the man from Yarraville.

George Tribe – the destroyer of Yorkshire in 1958 – warms up in the nets for the new season at Northamptonshire.

Northamptonshire won the toss and elected to field

Umpires: H Elliott & AEG Rhodes

YORKSHIRE

WB Stott	c Lightfoot b Tyson	3	b Manning	20
K Taylor	lbw b Tyson	0	c&b Manning	1
FA Lowson	c Allen b Tribe	7	c Manning b Tribe	16
DB Close	c Andrew b Tyson	46	lbw b Tribe	4
JV Wilson	c Subba Row b Tribe	1	lbw b Tribe	4
R Illingworth	c Norman b Tribe	0	c Brookes b Tribe	13
JR Burnet*	b Tribe	0	c Lightfoot b Tribe	3
JH Wardle	st Andrew b Tribe	0	c Brookes b Tribe	0
JG Binks+	b Tribe	3	b Tribe	0
D Pickles	b Tribe	0	c Tyson b Tribe	0
MJ Cowan	not out	0	not out	0
Extras	(b6 lb1)	7	(b1 lb3)	4
TOTAL		67		65

FOW 1st: 3,6,19,25,31,33,37,55,61
FOW 2nd: 18,33,43,47,48,52,52,56,65

Bowling 1st: Tyson 18.5-6-30-3 Lightfoot 11-7-8-0 Tribe 14-5-22-7

Bowling 2nd: Tyson 4-2-4-0 Lightfoot 3-0-11-0 Tribe 14.2-10-9-8 Manning 15-4-37-2

NORTHAMPTONSHIRE

D Brookes	c Close b Illingworth	18	c Taylor b Illingworth	9
AP Arnold	c Taylor b Illingworth	13	not out	13
BL Reynolds	c Taylor b Wardle	8	not out	3
MEJC Norman	c Cowan b Wardle	1		
R Subba Row*	b Wardle	21		
GE Tribe	b Wardle	10		
A Lightfoot	run out	9		
JS Manning	b Illingworth	4		
KV Andrew+	b Illingworth	0		
FH Tyson	not out	7		
MHJ Allen	lbw b Illingworth	6		
Extras	(b8 lb1 w1)	10	(b1 lb2)	3
TOTAL		107	(1 wkt)	28

FOW 1st: 30,33,34,47,66,86,86,90,91
FOW 2nd: 15

Bowling 1st: Pickles 2-0-9-0 Cowan 3-0-13-0 Wardle 25-9-38-4 Illingworth 23.2-9-37-5

Bowling 2nd: Wardle 4.1-1-10-0 Illingworth 4-0-15-1

NORTHAMPTONSHIRE WON BY 9 WICKETS

The Australians

19, 20, 21 July 1961 at Northampton

It remains one of Northamptonshire cricket's most enduring mysteries; why on earth didn't Albert Lightfoot run? Limited-overs conditioning would see any modern-day professional, installed at the non-striker's end with his team needing one to win off the last ball and the wicketkeeper (a makeshift wicketkeeper at that) standing back, set off for the single with the bowler in his delivery stride – earlier, if he could get away with it. But Lightfoot, the county's own Shropshire lad, stayed put. 'I can only think he didn't get his sums right,' recalls Keith Andrew, trying to shed some light on a still-baffling scenario.

The Australians came to play a side struggling badly in the 1961 County Championship; ten matches lost by the middle of July and their captain, Raman Subba Row, missing half the programme on international duty in what was to be his final season in the first-class game. But the tourists' confidence was none too robust either. They had been hammered in the Headingley Test a few days earlier and would go to Old Trafford the following week with the series level at one-all. David Larter, the county's towering fast bowler destined for England recognition in 1962, added to their woes by having Bill Lawry taken in the slips off the second ball of the game, without a run on the board. Norman O'Neill then counter-attacked and only just missed a century before lunch, but the experienced Colin McDonald went off with an injured wrist and 313 all out was not a formidable total on an easy-paced pitch. Mick Norman and Brian Reynolds, the Northampton/Kettering opening partnership formed the previous summer after the retirement of Dennis Brookes and Reynolds' return from a broken leg, launched Northamptonshire's reply with 128. Lightfoot looked set to emulate Alex Snowden (1934) and Brookes (1956) by taking a century off Australia until Subba Row declared 24 behind.

His enterprise was quickly rewarded. With McDonald and Wally Grout, who had gone down with a bad stomach, unable to bat, Richie Benaud's side slumped from 64 for one to 173 all out; only Lawry's fighting hundred keeping them in the match. Northamptonshire needed 198 in 145 minutes to lower the Aussies' colours for the first time in the club's history, and more positive batting from Norman and Lightfoot brought the requirement down to four off the last over, to be bowled by Alan Davidson, with six wickets in hand. The first two balls produced just a single; then Brian Crump was run out with three still needed. New batsman Malcolm Scott hit the next delivery for two, levelling the scores. He missed the next, which went through to Bobby Simpson who was deputising for Grout behind the stumps. It was one run from one ball. Scott again failed to make contact but set off for a bye; Lightfoot, as the whole world now knows, didn't. Keith Andrew's observation – 'Albert wasn't too popular, put it that way!' – smacks of an understatement. Nowadays, the theme to *The Great Escape* would have echoed around the ground as Benaud walked off the field, chuckling to himself.

Why didn't he run? Albert Lightfoot, hero and villain of the match.

Australians won the toss and elected to bat

Umpires: WH Copson & DJ Wood

AUSTRALIANS

WM Lawry	c Subba Row b Larter	0		c Andrew b Larter	100
RB Simpson	c&b Lightfoot	30		lbw b Larter	22
NC O'Neill	b Dilley	142		c Allen b Lightfoot	2
BC Booth	run out	16		c Lightfoot b Crump	16
CC McDonald	retired hurt	38		absent hurt	
AK Davidson	c Lightfoot b Dilley	3	(5)	c&b Scott	8
R Benaud*	run out	27	(6)	c Norman b Scott	15
ATW Grout	c&b Scott	49		absent hurt	
GD McKenzie	c Watts b Scott	6	(7)	c Larter b Allen	4
LF Kline	b Larter	0	(8)	c Andrew b Scott	0
RA Gaunt	not out	0	(9)	not out	1
Extras	(1b1 w1)	2		(1b4 w1)	5
TOTAL		313			173

FOW 1st: 0,81,145,221,231,298,312,313,313
FOW 2nd: 36,64,73,97,123,152,152,173

Bowling 1st: Larter 13.5-2-56-2 Dilley 17-2-64-2 Lightfoot 26-6-70-1 Allen 13-5-34-0 Crump 21-7-42-0 Scott 11-1-45-2

Bowling 2nd: Larter 12.3-3-34-2 Dilley 11-3-33-0 Lightfoot 9-1-21-1 Allen 14-7-23-1 Crump 16-10-18-1 Scott 17-6-39-3

NORTHAMPTONSHIRE

MEJC Norman	b Benaud	66	c sub b Davidson	84
BL Reynolds	c Kline b Davidson	60	b Davidson	2
PJ Watts	c Benaud b McKenzie	37	b Davidson	13
R Subba Row*	b McKenzie	5	c Booth b Benaud	33
A Lightfoot	not out	80	not out	57
BS Crump	b Gaunt	2	run out	3
ME Scott	lbw b Kline	12	run out	2
KV Andrew+	not out	12		
MHJ Allen				
MR Dilley				
JDF Larter				
Extras	(b7 1b2 w2 nb4)	15	(b2 w1)	3
TOTAL	(6 wkts dec)	289	(6 wkts)	197

FOW 1st: 128,136,143,211,218,263
FOW 2nd: 3,33,88,183,195,197

Bowling 1st: Davidson 20-8-26-1 Gaunt 17-2-48-1 Benaud 24-11-33-1 Kline 25-7-63-1 McKenzie 20-7-49-2 O'Neill 5-1-24-0 Simpson 8-0-31-0

Bowling 2nd: Davidson 14-1-42-3 Gaunt 6-0-24-0 Benaud 11-0-70-1 McKenzie 13-0-58-0

MATCH DRAWN

SUSSEX

10 July 1963 at Northampton

In the spring of 1962, Keith Andrew – peerless wicketkeeper and canny captain – led Northamptonshire to victory in the final of the Midlands Knock-Out Competition. It was, in effect, a 'dry run' for the inaugural Gillette Cup the following season, and the county won it with a five-wicket triumph over Leicestershire at Grace Road. The successful players each received a souvenir ashtray for their pains, but the true value of the experience gained only became clear in 1963, when Andrew's men reached the last four of the newfangled winner-takes-all tournament.

Warwickshire and Middlesex were dispatched comfortably enough in the early rounds, and Northamptonshire then welcomed Sussex to Wantage Road for the ground's first major 'one-day' occasion. The visiting team contained Ted Dexter and Jim Parks, both of whom travelled to Northampton from Birmingham where England had just hammered the West Indies by ten wickets in the Third Test. They were soon together in the middle as Sussex lost Alan Oakman, Richard Langridge and Ken Suttle for 49, and the pair received generous applause from the 5,000-strong crowd (paying a comparatively steep five shillings a time) in recognition of their efforts at Edgbaston. Slowly but surely, they wrested the initiative from Northamptonshire's bowlers, pushing sharp singles to unsettle the field and punishing anything loose.

Dexter had made 26 when the game's decisive moment arrived. Parks ran one down to third man where Brian Crump picked up and winged in an accurate return to Andrew as Dexter attempted to complete a third. Many spectators thought – and still think – that the England skipper failed to make his ground, but the umpire ruled otherwise. Dexter promptly moved up a gear to hit a six and 17 fours in his 115 (maintaining concentration when rain stopped play with his score on 99!), and he put on 160 for the fourth wicket with Parks to lay the foundations for a formidable total. Larter returned to wrap up the innings with a hat-trick – Cooper and Pountain with the last two balls of his fourteenth over, Tony Buss with the first ball of his fifteenth – but Sussex were practically out of sight already.

Northamptonshire's reply was doomed from a very early stage. Brian Reynolds departed to a sad run-out, and Dexter's catch to remove Colin Milburn cheaply killed off the home side's faint hopes of getting anywhere near. Roger Prideaux, who had achieved the distinction of becoming the county's first Man of the Match award-winner in the first round victory over Warwickshire, at least ensured respectability with 73, while Crump rounded off a handy all-round display as the tie drifted to its inevitable conclusion. All that remained was for Herbert Sutcliffe to give Dexter his gold medal and cheque for £50, leaving Northamptonshire to ponder – for the first, but not the last time in one-day cricket – on what might have been.

Flashback to a happier moment in the 1963 Gillette Cup campaign. Roger Prideaux receives the Man of the Match award from Frank Woolley, after first-round victory over Warwickshire.

Sussex won the toss and elected to bat

Umpires: JS Buller & AED Smith

SUSSEX

RJ Langridge	lbw b Watts	16
ASM Oakman	b Larter	0
KG Suttle	c Larter b Milburn	19
ER Dexter*	b Watts	115
JM Parks+	c Ramsamooj b Scott	71
LJ Lenham	b Crump	41
GC Cooper	b Larter	11
FR Pountain	b Larter	0
NI Thomson	run out	1
A Buss	b Larter	1
DL Bates	not out	0
Extras	(b4 lb8 nb5)	17
TOTAL		292

FOW: 1,33,49,209,250,285,285,291,292

Bowling: Larter 14.1-0-68-4 Crump 14-2-46-1 Watts 14-1-50-2 Milburn 13-0-80-1 Scott 7-0-31-1

NORTHAMPTONSHIRE

MEJC Norman	b Thomson	21
BL Reynolds	run out	2
C Milburn	c Dexter b Bates	6
RM Prideaux	c Cooper b Buss	73
PJ Watts	b Thomson	3
A Lightfoot	b Dexter	3
D Ramsamooj	b Dexter	21
BS Crump	not out	34
KV Andrew*+	b Thomson	4
ME Scott	lbw b Dexter	4
JDF Larter	c Lenham b Thomson	2
Extras	(b1 lb8 nb5)	14
TOTAL		187

FOW: 7,26,44,48,69,118,160,170,178

Bowling: Thomson 13.3-2-33-4 Bates 15-2-63-1 Buss 11-1-32-1 Dexter 9-0-40-3 Pountain 1-0-5-0

SUSSEX WON BY 105 RUNS

GLAMORGAN

4, 5, 6 August 1965 at Cardiff

The town of Northampton had never known such sporting times. In March 1965, the Northampton Saints winger Andy Hancock ran from his own 25 to score one of the great Calcutta Cup tries, earning England a last-gasp draw with the Scots at Twickenham. The following month, supporters of Northampton Town – The Cobblers – were celebrating promotion into English football's top flight under the shrewd management of Dave Bowen. And by August, Northamptonshire's cricketers were mounting a promising challenge for the County Championship title. The match against fellow contenders Glamorgan in Cardiff was likely to prove crucial in determining the final outcome.

Keith Andrew's team boasted precious few 'stars'. At the start of the season, its only Test players were David Larter and the captain himself with nine appearances between them (although Larter made another three in 1965). Colin Milburn would gain England honours a year later and Roger Prideaux in 1968, but David Steele's brief, glorious brush with international fame was still a decade away. The other regulars – Brian Reynolds and Mick Norman, Peter and Jim Watts, Brian Crump and Albert Lightfoot, plus the two front-line spinners, Haydn Sully and Malcolm Scott – were all genuine county professionals; roundheads rather than cavaliers.

Without a single Championship point until the last week of May, Northamptonshire's bid for honours began with a win over Warwickshire. Eight more victories sent them to the Arms Park in confident mood, and once there it soon became apparent that a high-scoring contest was out of the question. From 29 for three, the county rallied through Prideaux and Steele who added 86 for the fourth wicket either side of lunch. The Watts brothers also dug in for a time, and although Don Shepherd – as usual – begrudged the batsmen each and every run, Northamptonshire's 186 all out

Northamptonshire's 1965 team – runners-up to Worcestershire by only four points. From left to right, standing: M.E. Scott, H. Sully, P.J. Watts, P.D. Watts, C. Milburn, D.S. Steele, B.S. Crump. Seated: A. Lightfoot, R.M. Prideaux, K.V. Andrew (captain), B.L. Reynolds. Insets: M.E. Kettle, J.D.F. Larter.

The first three captains to lead Northamptonshire to second place in the County Championship: Keith Andrew (1965), 'Tubby' Vials (1912) and Dennis Brookes (1957).

seemed only a little below par for the conditions. But Glamorgan snatched a narrow lead, thanks to an irritating last wicket stand of 31 between Shepherd and Ossie Wheatley, and a dismal second-day collapse left the visitors in dire straits at 32 for six, only 29 in front.

Jim Watts' Northamptonshire career lasted, with two breaks, until 1980, and in all that time he played few more vital innings than this one against the Welshmen. His dogged 51, with game support from Crump and Lightfoot, at least gave the county attack something to bowl at, and welcome rain on Thursday night made Glamorgan's task of scoring 139 for victory that much more testing, especially against Crump – described by Neville Cardus that year as 'the insidious seamer'. The all-rounder from Staffordshire, Steele's cousin, had a dressing-room reputation as an 'aches-and-pains player' who would regale team-mates, and his captain, with a catalogue of ailments, before going out and trundling all day. On this particular Friday, 'The Atomic Pill' bowled unchanged to bring his tally of overs in the match to 76. With Lightfoot, who sent down only that many overs all season, capturing three key wickets in the middle order, Northamptonshire reduced Glamorgan to 77 for six at lunch; then Crump ran out Euros Lewis with a direct hit. It was all over at 3.20 p.m., and the county were eighteen points clear at the top of the table.

A few days later, the club's committee discussed what should be done if the Championship was secured. There was wild talk of a civic reception. Did anyone know where to hire open-top buses from? But the rest of the story is almost too painful to relate: defeat at the hands of Worcestershire, who then beat Hampshire at Bournemouth in a still-controversial match of three declarations; and rain in Northampton, when a win over Gloucestershire was imperative to keep the title hopes alive. Northamptonshire lost out to Worcestershire by four points in the final table, and have never come as close to glory since. Oh, and the Cobblers were relegated at the end of the season.

Jim Watts.

Northamptonshire won the toss and elected to bat

Umpires: PA Gibb & JG Langridge

NORTHAMPTONSHIRE

MEJC Norman	lbw b Wheatley	4	b Miller		3
BL Reynolds	c&b Wheatley	9	c Miller b Shepherd		14
C Milburn	c EJ Lewis b Shepherd	16	c Presdee b Miller		0
RM Prideaux	c Walker b Shepherd	40	b Miller		2
DS Steele	lbw b EJ Lewis	55	b Shepherd		0
PJ Watts	b Shepherd	26	c Walker b Shepherd		51
BS Crump	c Hedges b Shepherd	5	lbw b Presdee		31
PD Watts	c&b Wheatley	25	c Evans b Shepherd		10
A Lightfoot	c EJ Lewis b Shepherd	0	c Walker b Shepherd		17
ME Scott	c Walker b Shepherd	1	c Walker b Presdee		3
KV Andrew*+	not out	0	not out		0
Extras	(lb3 nb2)	5	(b4 lb6)		10
TOTAL		186			141

FOW 1st: 8,15,29,115,139,144,164,166,186
FOW 2nd: 13,13,19,19,19,32,78,131,139

Bowling 1st: Wheatley 16.3-9-16-3 Miller 15-5-45-0 Shepherd 34-20-32-6 Presdee 10-3-20-0 EJ Lewis 24-8-68-1

Bowling 2nd: Wheatley 9-6-23-0 Miller 12-4-21-3 Shepherd 31-15-51-5 Presdee 11.3-5-14-2 EJ Lewis 8-3-22-0

GLAMORGAN

B Hedges	lbw b Steele	47	c PD Watts b Crump	12
A Jones	st Andrew b Scott	21	c Andrew b PJ Watts	13
PM Walker	c&b PJ Watts	55	lbw b Lightfoot	10
HDS Miller	c Steele b Crump	1	c Steele b Lightfoot	1
AR Lewis	c Reynolds b PJ Watts	20	c Milburn b Lightfoot	15
JS Presdee	c Steele b PJ Watts	0	c Steele b Crump	2
A Rees	c PD Watts b Crump	2	lbw b Crump	37
EJ Lewis	c Steele b PJ Watts	0	run out	2
DGL Evans+	lbw b Crump	3	lbw b Crump	9
DJ Shepherd	not out	22	c Prideaux b Scott	9
OS Wheatley*	b Crump	10	not out	0
Extras	(lb6 nb2)	8	(b4 lb6)	10
TOTAL		189		120

FOW 1st: 27,83,84,129,133,138,143,150,158
FOW 2nd: 22,26,36,54,57,77,79,86,115

Bowling 1st: Crump 41.2-15-77-4 PJ Watts 28-9-43-4 Scott 13-5-43-1 Steele 10-4-18-1

Bowling 2nd: Crump 35.1-11-65-4 PJ Watts 15-4-17-1 Scott 1-0-4-1 Lightfoot 20-8-24-3

NORTHAMPTONSHIRE WON BY 18 RUNS

ESSEX

17, 18, 19 August 1966 at Clacton-on-Sea

Allan Lamb acquired the pleasing habit of taking out his frustration with the England selectors on the next county attack he happened to come up against. This was not, however, a new phenomenon in Northamptonshire circles. Colin Milburn made Essex pay a heavy price for the perceived folly of Messrs Insole, Bedser, Kenyon and May on a never-to-be-forgotten August day at the seaside, in the summer of Geoff Hurst and Kenneth Wolstenholme.

Milburn's explosive power at the crease, his entertainment value both on and off the field and, later, his tremendous courage in adversity made him the 'Cricketer Most Admired' of a whole generation of county supporters. His appearance on the international stage in 1966 widened that appeal. Run out for a duck on his debut against the West Indies at Old Trafford, he hit 94 in the second innings, followed by a maiden century at Lord's where the attempt by spectators to lift him shoulder-high in triumph was decidedly over-optimistic. He was less successful at Trent Bridge and Headingley but still averaged 52.66 in his first four Tests. So they dropped him.

Comments in the press suggested that Milburn's bulk was the deciding factor. Too slow in the field, the selectors reckoned. The fact that he had proved himself an outstanding close fielder in county cricket (with 43 catches in 1964, still a Northamptonshire record) clearly escaped their attention. 'Ollie' heard the news on the Sunday of a Championship match against Leicestershire, and the *Northamptonshire Evening Telegraph* dutifully recorded his two-word reaction: 'Blow Me!' Skipper Keith Andrew, writing a column in the same newspaper, stormed: 'I am really angry about this.'

Three days later, he went in first with Roger Prideaux at Clacton to face a perfectly respectable Essex attack, comprising England all-rounder Barry Knight, fellow seamers Tony Jorden and Brian Edmeades, and the spin of Robin Hobbs and David Acfield.

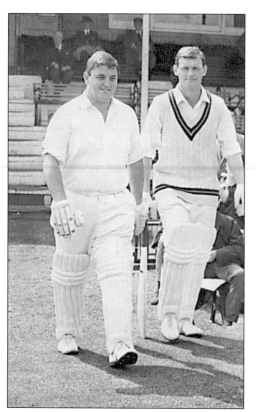

As Milburn recalled later, 'Roger gave me most of the strike when he saw the mood I was in.' It was a shrewd move by the vice-captain. The disgruntled Geordie smashed a hundred before lunch and was out by teatime for 203 in 250 minutes, including 4 big sixes and 22 fours. The opening partnership of 293 was Northamptonshire's highest in Championship cricket – it beat the 243 posted by Dennis Brookes and Percy Davis at Kidderminster in 1946 and would stand for another thirty years.

After Andrew's overnight declaration, Essex struggled against Haydn Sully's off-breaks and followed on 179 behind. Malcolm Scott, slow left-arm, did the damage second time around, leaving Northamptonshire requiring 55 to win. Milburn and Prideaux, with 356 runs between them in the first knock, both went for nought before Mushtaq Mohammad saw it through. Not even W.S. Gilbert could have devised a more 'Topsy-Turvy' storyline.

Northamptonshire's record-breaking openers, who posted 293 against Essex at Clacton in 1966 – Colin Milburn and Roger Prideaux.

Northamptonshire won the toss and elected to bat

Umpires: A Jepson & H Yarnold

NORTHAMPTONSHIRE

C Milburn	c Bear b Acfield	203	c&b Knight	0
RM Prideaux	not out	153	c Knight b Jorden	0
BL Reynolds	c Fletcher b Hobbs	4	c Knight b Barker	18
Mushtaq Mohammad	not out	42	not out	31
DS Steele			not out	4
PJ Watts				
BS Crump				
ME Scott				
KV Andrew*+				
H Sully				
AJ Durose				
Extras	(lb10 nb1)	11	(lb2 nb1)	3
TOTAL	(2 wkts dec)	413	(3 wkts)	56

FOW 1st: 293,308
FOW 2nd: 0,0,48

Bowling 1st: Knight 25-4-69-0 Jorden 11-1-62-0 Edmeades 19-1-77-0 Hobbs 30-3-94-1 Acfield 23-3-99-1 Barker 1-0-1-0

Bowling 2nd: Knight 5-2-12-1 Jorden 8-0-35-1 Hobbs 2-0-6-0 Barker 1-1-0-1

ESSEX

GJ Saville	c Andrew b Durose	29	c Watts b Mushtaq	22
MJ Bear	c Watts b Durose	3	c Steele b Sully	65
G Barker*	c Milburn b Sully	34	lbw b Scott	23
KWR Fletcher	c Watts b Sully	24	c Watts b Scott	41
B Taylor+	lbw b Sully	43	c Steele b Scott	20
BR Knight	c Andrew b Sully	2	c Sully b Scott	22
GR Cass	c Watts b Sully	29	c Reynolds b Scott	4
BEA Edmeades	lbw b Sully	47	c Watts b Durose	8
RNS Hobbs	b Crump	4	b Crump	16
AM Jorden	c Andrew b Sully	4	not out	7
DL Acfield	not out	0	lbw b Crump	0
Extras	(b6 lb4 nb5)	15	(b2 lb1 w1 nb1)	5
TOTAL		234		233

FOW 1st: 5,68,68,112,136,149,203,215,220
FOW 2nd: 42,86,122,122,157,190,207,222,233

Bowling 1st: Crump 29-8-47-1 Durose 11-1-36-2 Watts 11-4-26-0 Sully 36-12-69-7 Mushtaq 8-2-15-0 Scott 17-6-26-0

Bowling 2nd: Crump 9.4-1-28-2 Durose 8-2-14-1 Sully 16-2-69-1 Mushtaq 10-4-21-1 Scott 33-9-69-5 Steele 8-1-27-0

NORTHAMPTONSHIRE WON BY 7 WICKETS

THE WEST INDIANS

21, 22, 23 May 1969 at Northampton

Northamptonshire's record against touring sides from the Caribbean in the 1960s bears the closest scrutiny. Rain on the last day prevented a likely victory over Frank Worrell's team in 1963, Colin Milburn introducing himself to the West Indians with memorable innings of 100 and 88. Three years later, Gary Sobers' men were dispatched by four wickets inside two days, reviving happy memories of 1933. So when Sobers returned to Wantage Road in 1969, he at least knew what to expect.

Milburn was again to the fore, cracking nine fours in his 41 out of a 59-run opening partnership with Roger Prideaux, who went on to top-score with 79. But from a prosperous-looking 187 for three, Northamptonshire collapsed against the pace of Grayson Shillingford; his burst of five wickets in 13 balls – removing Prideaux, Hylton Ackerman, Brian Crump, Sarfraz Nawaz and wicketkeeper Laurie Johnson – left the county tottering at 199 for eight before David Steele came to the rescue, adding 64 for the last two wickets in the company of Haydn Sully and Tony Durose.

The tourists were batting on the first evening and quickly fell foul of Durose, the Cheshire-born fast bowler who had destroyed Leicestershire (to the immense satisfaction of all true Northamptonians) with a career-best 7-23 at Peterborough the previous season, dismissing the visitors for 43. This time, Durose shattered Steve Camacho's stumps with the third ball of his opening over, and had Charlie Davis caught behind off the next. Basil Butcher saved the hat-trick, but the West Indies trailed by 117 and a bright half-century from Mushtaq Mohammad, signed after the Pakistan Eaglets tour of 1963 but only now qualified for Championship cricket, set up Prideaux's declaration.

The target was 300, and at 201 for four it seemed that Northamptonshire might come unstuck. With Brian Crump in the team? Never. He settled the issue with a spell of four for nine in 27 balls, including Sobers (suffering with a heavy cold) for nought, and the last five wickets tumbled for 33 with the injured Joey Carew unable to bat. The cricketing world had learned that 1966 was no flash in the pan.

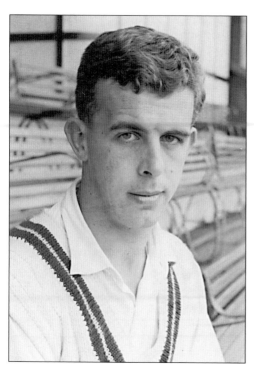

For Milburn, the season was panning out perfectly. His knock of 139 in Karachi just three months earlier had, surely, cemented his England place for the foreseeable future, and he followed up with 158 in the opening Championship match against Leicestershire. Now the West Indians had been beaten. But that same Friday night, 23 May 1969, 'Ollie' was involved in a car crash at Moulton, near Northampton, and lost his left eye. A couple of days later, his team-mates were defeated in a John Player League match at Lord's and *Wisden* recorded: 'In the weekend of Colin Milburn's accident, Northamptonshire seemed to have little heart for cricket.' It was hardly surprising.

Tony Durose.

Northamptonshire won the toss and elected to bat

Umpires: JS Buller & CS Elliott

NORTHAMPTONSHIRE

C Milburn	b Holder	41	lbw b Shillingford		6
RM Prideaux*	b Shillingford	79	c Camacho b Roberts		31
A Lightfoot	c Sobers b Roberts	25	b Shillingford		5
Mushtaq Mohammad	c Carew b Foster	42	c Findlay b Holder		51
HM Ackerman	c Findlay b Shillingford	0	c Findlay b Shillingford		23
DS Steele	not out	33	b Roberts		23
BS Crump	c Carew b Shillingford	0	lbw b Holder		2
Sarfraz Nawaz	lbw b Shillingford	0	b Holder		5
LA Johnson+	lbw b Shillingford	4	b Roberts		1
H Sully	c Findlay b Davis	10	not out		2
AJ Durose	b Davis	16	not out		24
Extras	(lb9 nb4)	13	(lb8 nb1)		9
TOTAL		263	(9 wkts dec)		182

FOW 1st: 59,103,187,188,195,195,195,199,233
FOW 2nd: 16,30,75,116,141,149,151,155,156

Bowling 1st: Holder 19-2-61-1 Shillingford 20-2-79-5 Davis 21.2-6-38-2 Roberts 28-9-61-1 Foster 6-1-11-1

Bowling 2nd: Holder 18-4-40-3 Shillingford 18-7-43-3 Davis 10-2-31-0 Roberts 24-7-59-3

WEST INDIANS

GS Camacho	b Durose	0	run out		87
MLC Foster	lbw b Mushtaq	61	b Sarfraz		1
CA Davis	c Johnson b Durose	0	b Crump		57
BF Butcher	c Prideaux b Sarfraz	35	not out		41
CH Lloyd	run out	1	c Milburn b Crump		29
GS Sobers*	b Durose	16	b Crump		0
TM Findlay+	c&b Mushtaq	0	c Ackerman b Mushtaq		13
VA Holder	not out	15	lbw b Crump		0
P Roberts	c Milburn b Sarfraz	4	run out		0
GC Shillingford	b Sarfraz	9	b Sarfraz		0
MC Carew	absent hurt		absent hurt		
Extras	(lb4 nb1)	5	(b1 lb5)		6
TOTAL		146			234

FOW 1st: 0,0,45,46,116,116,117,134,146
FOW 2nd: 3,75,138,182,201,215,215,234,234

Bowling 1st: Durose 12-6-28-3 Sarfraz 15.3-2-52-3 Mushtaq 17-3-53-2 Sully 2-0-8-0

Bowling 2nd: Durose 16-6-36-0 Sarfraz 16.3-7-34-2 Mushtaq 26-9-92-1 Sully 3-1-11-0 Steele 13-3-27-0 Crump 17-8-28-4

NORTHAMPTONSHIRE WON BY 65 RUNS

THE AUSTRALIANS

5, 7, 8 August 1972 at Northampton

Ninety years after 'The Demon' discomfited Jim Kingston's men on the Racecourse, Northamptonshire exacted welcome, if belated revenge. The 1972 Australians, under Ian Chappell, were embroiled in an absorbing series with Ray Illingworth's England side, and trailed by two victories to one ahead of the final Test at The Oval, for which a sixth day had been scheduled if required. The Ashes would remain in the old country, but the rubber could be halved. As in 1930, it was not difficult to understand the tourists' mind-set; their thoughts on Kennington rather than Wantage Road. The difference was that Bill Woodfull's team got away with it.

The county, with Jim Watts in charge, were enjoying their best Championship season since Keith Andrew's retirement, boosted by a high-quality trio of bowling imports – Bob Cottam from Hampshire, John Dye from Kent and the Indian left-arm spinner Bishan Bedi. It was Bedi who claimed the first-day honours after Watts put the Australians in, triggering a slump from 104 for three shortly after lunch to 191 all out. By Saturday's close, Northamptonshire had reached 89 for two in reply – twenty-year-old Geoff Cook, playing his first match for a fortnight after injury, and Mushtaq Mohammad in possession. Sunday's John Player League match against Sussex at leafy Brackley was rained off, but play began promptly on Monday morning with the third-wicket pair looking to press home the advantage.

They carried the total to 142 before Cook was stumped off the 'mystery spinner', Johnny Gleeson, who removed Watts for a duck in the same over. Although Bob Massie, the hero of that summer's Lord's Test and a Northamptonshire Second XI player just two years earlier, was struggling with a neck problem, and Chappell used Dennis Lillee only sparingly, the Australians were able to restrict the county's advantage to 19 as Mushtaq ran out of partners. Graeme Watson had done the damage with his fiddly medium-pace, and he proceeded to give his side the upper hand with a sensible half-century. At 99 for two they led by 80, only for Bedi to prompt another collapse with the assistance of two catches and a stumping from the genial Laurie Johnson, then nearly thirty-six and making his final first-class appearance.

Northamptonshire began their second innings on Tuesday morning needing 125 to beat an Australian side for the first time. With Massie unable to bowl, David Steele – of whom Chappell and Co. would see a good deal more on their next trip – and Mushtaq made the game safe. When the Pakistani fell to Lillee, Watts sent in Brian Crump, like Johnson nearing the end of his distinguished career with Northamptonshire, to be present with his cousin at the kill. A nice thought, but somebody lost the script and Crump was run out with 21 still needed. In the event, Watts joined Steele in the match-winning partnership, the latter taking 15 runs off five balls from David Colley

David Steele.

(operating at something less than full-tilt) to make history a few minutes before lunch.

Northamptonshire were triumphant: 'The greatest moment since I became captain', according to Watts. Chappell was unimpressed with the pitch, but the *Sydney Sun* took the skipper to task for 'condoning the circus which blighted the concluding stages of the match.' Losing was bad enough, their reporter averred, 'but to show we didn't really care about it (was) enough to make even the most ardent cricket-hater squirm.' It was left to county secretary Ken Turner, in a tone of voice that brooked no argument, to sum up the situation: 'The better team won.'

Northamptonshire won the toss and elected to field

Umpires: J Arnold & WE Phillipson

AUSTRALIANS

BC Francis	lbw b Dye	27		b Dye	9
R Edwards	c Cottam b Willey	18		c Cook b Dye	8
IM Chappell*	b Willey	5		run out	31
GD Watson	c Crump b Bedi	37		hit wicket b Bedi	52
RW Marsh	c Willey b Crump	42		c Johnson b Bedi	0
RJ Inverarity	c Cottam b Bedi	14		lbw b Dye	6
DJ Colley	b Willey	1		c Johnson b Bedi	16
HB Taber+	c&b Bedi	28		st Johnson b Bedi	3
JW Gleeson	lbw b Bedi	5		b Willey	11
RAL Massie	not out	3		absent hurt	
DK Lillee	c Cottam b Bedi	0	(10)	not out	1
Extras	(b4 lb4 w1 nb2)	11		(b1 lb5)	6
TOTAL		191			143

FOW 1st: 32,50,50,104,140,141,158,175,191
FOW 2nd: 11,18,99,103,104,124,128,141,143

Bowling 1st: Cottam 12-5-27-0 Dye 14-3-42-1 Willey 18-3-47-3 Bedi 17-3-57-5 Crump 7-3-7-1

Bowling 2nd: Cottam 8-1-32-0 Dye 13-6-25-3 Willey 13.3-5-27-1 Bedi 20-6-53-4

NORTHAMPTONSHIRE

A Tait	b Massie	0			
G Cook	st Taber b Gleeson	62	(1)	c Chappell b Gleeson	24
DS Steele	lbw b Massie	19	(2)	not out	60
Mushtaq Mohammad	not out	88	(3)	c Marsh b Lillee	30
PJ Watts*	lbw b Gleeson	0		not out	3
BS Crump	lbw b Watson	3	(4)	run out	1
P Willey	lbw b Watson	8			
RMH Cottam	st Marsh b Gleeson	0			
LA Johnson+	b Watson	0			
BS Bedi	b Watson	4			
JCJ Dye	b Watson	4			
Extras	(b1 lb1 w1 nb19)	22		(lb1 nb6)	7
TOTAL		210		(3 wkts)	125

FOW 1st: 1,53,142,142,149,171,178,191,195
FOW 2nd: 38,103,104

Bowling 1st: Massie 24-10-50-2 Lillee 12-2-35-0 Colley 9-2-29-0 Watson 14-3-36-5 Gleeson 11-1-38-3

Bowling 2nd: Lillee 7-0-25-1 Colley 6.5-2-27-0 Watson 4-0-11-0 Gleeson 9-4-26-1 Inverarity 6-0-29-0

NORTHAMPTONSHIRE WON BY 7 WICKETS

LANCASHIRE
19 May 1974 at Northampton

The new 40-over John Player League, introduced in 1969, brought a certain amount of excitement but hardly any success to Northamptonshire in its first five years. The county's best showing was thirteenth place in 1970, and by 1973 they had sunk to the bottom of the one-day table, with only four victories all summer. Against Lancashire, acknowledged masters of the shorter game in the early 1970s, Northamptonshire went under in four of their first five Sunday meetings, managing a solitary win in a rain-shortened contest at Peterborough in 1972.

On the positive side, Lancashire's limited-overs prowess made them attractive visitors. The 1974 John Player fixture list brought David Lloyd's outfit to Wantage Road for Northamptonshire's second match of the season and, not surprisingly, skipper Jim Watts chose it as his benefit game. Happily for him, the fact that his team had lost to Somerset the week before didn't keep the spectators away.

They witnessed a controversial incident early in proceedings when Peter Willey, opening the innings, was run out backing up by the England fast bowler Peter Lever. 'I hated doing it,' Lever was quoted as saying in the *Daily Express*, 'but the fact is that I twice warned Willey about breaking too early. He was going about two or three yards down the wicket.' Umpire Tom Spencer had no option but to send Willey, a future member of the Test panel, on his way.

Suitably galvanised, Northamptonshire took charge of the match. The adaptable Watts moved himself up the order to number three, and the ploy paid off as he and Roy Virgin made steady progress against a Lancashire attack including the only Northamptonshire-born player in the match, Peter Lee. A late surge from David Steele – not, on the face of it, a natural for the 'hit-and-giggle' stuff – ensured a final total that was respectable at the very least, and potentially rather better than that, and granted Northamptonshire an early breakthrough.

It duly came when John Dye removed Ken Snellgrove, and the left-armer then joined forces with Sarfraz Nawaz to undermine Lancashire's reply. Sarfraz struck the most telling blow, having the always-dangerous Clive Lloyd caught behind for a single; soon half the side was out for 78, and not even Lancashire's renowned depth of batting could save them. Mushtaq Mohammad's leg-breaks and googlies finished the job, leaving Watts with two good reasons to be cheerful – a decent crowd to swell the benefit coffers, and probably Northamptonshire's best effort in the competition to date.

Nor was this to prove a one-off, as the team went on to notch ten wins in '74 and finish a vertiginous fourth. Even more significantly, nine of the players who saw off Lancashire that Sunday afternoon were on duty against the same opposition at Lord's a couple of years later. And they had learned that the men from Old Trafford were not invincible.

Jim Watts, who scored vital runs in his benefit match.

Northamptonshire won the toss and elected to bat

Umpires: TW Spencer & JG Langridge

NORTHAMPTONSHIRE

RT Virgin	b Wood	53
P Willey	run out	1
PJ Watts*	c Hughes b CH Lloyd	61
Mushtaq Mohammad	b Sullivan	10
G Sharp+	run out	1
DS Steele	run out	34
Sarfraz Nawaz	c Lyon b Sullivan	0
W Larkins	c Sullivan b CH Lloyd	11
A Hodgson	run out	11
RMH Cottam	not out	1
JCJ Dye	not out	0
Extras	(b1 lb11 nb3)	15
TOTAL	(9 wkts)	198

FOW: 29,94,131,131,133,140,154,195,197

Bowling: Lever 8-0-35-0 Lee 5-0-33-0 Simmons 5-0-32-0 Wood 8-0-27-1 Sulliva 8-0-39-2 CH Lloyd 5-0-17-2

LANCASHIRE

D Lloyd*	b Dye	18
KL Snellgrove	c Mushtaq b Dye	4
FC Hayes	b Sarfraz	38
CH Lloyd	c Sharp b Sarfraz	1
J Sullivan	c&b Hodgson	2
DP Hughes	b Mushtaq	22
B Wood	c&b Mushtaq	13
J Simmons	b Hodgson	11
J Lyon+	b Mushtaq	9
P Lever	c Dye b Mushtaq	6
PG Lee	not out	3
Extras	(b2 lb4 w1 nb5)	12
TOTAL		139

FOW: 7,46,47,52,78,97,112,120,127

Bowling: Cottam 6-0-14-0 Dye 8-1-21-2 Sarfraz 8-1-22-2 Hodgson 8-0-40-2 Mushtaq 5.5-0-30-4

NORTHAMPTONSHIRE WON BY 59 RUNS

I AM NO CHEAT
SAYS LEVER
Lancashire bowler in run-out rumpus

ESSEX

3, 5, 6 August 1974 at Leyton

Northamptonshire's annual report for 1974 admitted, somewhat coyly, to 'a certain amount of satisfaction' at the team's showing during the season. Of their nine Championship victories, none was more eventful nor more tense than the two-run triumph over Essex, secured barely five minutes into the final day's play. If some of the players spent a sleepless Monday night, at least they were rewarded the following morning with 17 points and the opportunity to make an early start to the next fixture, in distant Blackpool.

Northamptonshire's first innings was a workaday affair, built around a solid century from Roy Virgin. In his first full summer with Northamptonshire after heading north from Somerset, Virgin hit seven hundreds in the Championship – of which this was the fifth – and fell just short of 2,000 first-class runs, giving the county some greatly-needed stability at the top of the order. Until his arrival, so much had depended on David Steele and Mushtaq Mohammad at three and four; now they tended to come together less frequently at 10 for two inside the first half-hour.

The fourth bonus point was missed by a single run, but that minor disappointment was soon forgotten as Essex declined from 61 without loss overnight to present the visitors with a handy lead of 94, Bishan Bedi and John Dye taking the bowling honours. By this time, rain had done its work on the pitch and Northamptonshire found no answer to the left-arm spin of Ray East, who shared the new ball with Keith Boyce, and Stuart Turner's nagging seamers. Despite a good start, courtesy of Virgin and Alan Tait, the last nine wickets crashed for 43. Essex needed 170 to win, and were in good enough shape at 160 for six to prompt Keith Fletcher to claim the extra half-hour on the second evening.

But Jim Watts kept encouraging his bowlers and his optimism was rewarded with three quick

wickets – two for Alan Hodgson, one for Bedi – to leave the home team on 167 for nine when time ran out. A total of 29 wickets had fallen in the day for 386 runs, and not a pitch liaison officer in sight. Then, the moving ball was regarded as a challenge to technique rather than an affront to nature. One delivery could now decide the match one way or the other. In this war of nerves, which side would blink first?

Bob Cottam resumed the attack on Tuesday against John Lever, who immediately edged to slip where Virgin spilled the chance. It had all the makings of 'one of those days.' Or did it? Watts turned to Bedi at the other end, and the Indian's first ball had Robin Hobbs smartly held by Geoff Cook in the gully. Northamptonshire had shaded it; now for the long drive to Blackpool, noted for fresh air and fun.

Bishan Bedi.

Essex v. Northamptonshire

Northamptonshire won the toss and elected to bat

Umpires: WE Alley & JF Crapp

NORTHAMPTONSHIRE

Batsman	1st innings		2nd innings	
RT Virgin	b Turner	106	c Boyce b East	13
A Tait	c Smith b Lever	16	c McEwan b Turner	20
DS Steele	c Smith b Edmeades	22	c Lever b East	17
G Cook	b Hobbs	42	c Boyce b East	9
P Willey	b Boyce	32	c Hobbs b East	6
PJ Watts*	c Smith b Lever	23	c Smith b Turner	1
G Sharp+	not out	19	c Smith b East	1
A Hodgson	run out	18	c Hardie b Turner	1
RMH Cottam	run out	0	c&b Turner	2
BS Bedi	run out	6	b Turner	0
JCJ Dye			not out	1
Extras	(b3 lb4 nb8)	15	(nb4)	4
TOTAL	(9 wkts)	299		75

FOW 1st: 28,80,189,201,247,255,280,282,299
FOW 2nd: 32,39,40,53,66,67,68,68,71

Bowling 1st: Boyce 30-5-105-1 Lever 18-1-49-2 Turner 15-1-37-1 Edmeades 7-2-14-1 East 18-3-46-0 Hobbs 12-4-33-1

Bowling 2nd: Boyce 6-0-24-0 East 16.4-6-27-5 Turner 12-4-20-5

ESSEX

Batsman	1st innings		2nd innings	
BEA Edmeades	c Sharp b Dye	22	c&b Hodgson	33
BR Hardie	c Virgin b Dye	50	c Cook b Steele	30
KS McEwan	c Watts b Steele	27	c Virgin b Bedi	4
KWR Fletcher*	b Dye	0	c Sharp b Cottam	24
RMO Cooke	c Sharp b Cottam	0	c Steele b Hodgson	1
S Turner	c Cook b Bedi	47	c Cook b Hodgson	14
KD Boyce	c Steele b Bedi	9	b Bedi	31
RE East	c Virgin b Bedi	4	c Dye b Hodgson	22
N Smith+	c Tait b Dye	31	c Watts b Hodgson	1
RNS Hobbs	c Watts b Steele	0	c Cook b Bedi	1
JK Lever	not out	12	not out	1
Extras	(nb3)	3	(b1 nb4)	5
TOTAL		205		167

FOW 1st: 68,79,79,82,109,124,130,171,178
FOW 2nd: 54,56,70,113,128,130,160,165,165

Bowling 1st: Cottam 15-2-60-1 Dye 13.1-2-44-4 Bedi 19-9-45-3 Steele 14-2-53-2

Bowling 2nd: Cottam 9-3-30-1 Dye 3-1-13-0 Bedi 17.1-1-72-3 Hodgson 15-6-36-5 Steele 4-0-11-1

NORTHAMPTONSHIRE WON BY 2 RUNS

LANCASHIRE

4 September 1976 at Lord's

When, in 1904, Northamptonshire clinched the Minor Counties Championship title, the modest celebrations might well have been even more muted had Tom Horton, Lord Lilford, 'Pat' Darnell and the club's other stalwarts of the period realised that a seventy-two-year wait lay in store before the county would win anything else. Late in 1974, it was suggested in committee that an 'Honours Board' should be erected in memory of 'Tubby' Vials. A few puzzled expressions around the table swiftly prompted the explanation that this would carry the names of past chairmen and presidents, rather than list Northamptonshire's non-existent triumphs. The tired old jokes about cobwebs in the trophy cabinet had gone a long way past their sell-by date, and in 1976 they were finally consigned to the dustbin of history.

Just as the appearance of Halley's Comet in 1910 signalled Northamptonshire's first Championship win over Yorkshire, so the great drought of '76 gave notice that another sensation was in the offing. Victories over Nottinghamshire and Hertfordshire propelled Mushtaq Mohammad's side into the Gillette Cup semi-finals, where Hampshire were overcome by two wickets in a horribly tense finish – so tense, indeed, that secretary Ken Turner claimed to have smoked his way through seventy-two Senior Service cigarettes during the afternoon. But at the end of it all, Northamptonshire were into a Lord's final for the first time. Lancashire, the cup holders, would provide the opposition.

David Steele, in the latter stages of his 'national hero' phase, had been controversially left out at Southampton, but returned to the ranks for the big one and was soon celebrating with the rest as John Dye flattened Farokh Engineer's leg stump with the seventh ball of the morning. Then, in his fifth over, Dye pinned Barry Wood on the right hand and the key all-rounder played no further part in the match. Despite useful contributions from David Lloyd and

A trophy at last! Mushtaq Mohammad takes possession of the Gillette Cup.

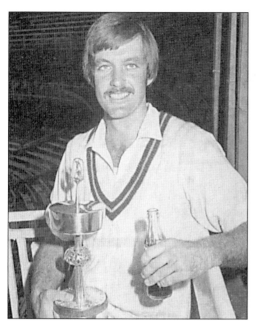

Man of the Match, Peter Willey, with the Gillette Cup and liquid refreshment.

John Dye's contribution to victory was impossible to over-estimate: the wicket of Farokh Engineer and the removal of Barry Wood.

John Abrahams, Lancashire reached the final over on 169 for seven – well below par, surely.

Concerned that Dye might be too stiff after a longish absence from the attack, Mushtaq called up Bishan Bedi to send down the last six balls of the innings. The striker, David Hughes, had earned a place in Gillette Cup folklore with his late-night batting heroics in the 1971 semi-final against Gloucestershire, but it was highly unlikely that lightning would strike twice. Except that it did. Hughes slammed Bedi for 26 precious runs – 4, 6, 2, 2, 6, 6 – and the red rose was rampant again.

Northamptonshire's response began cautiously. Roy Virgin and Peter Willey managed only 19 off the first ten overs from the two Peters, Lever and Lee, but timed their acceleration to perfection and sent up the century partnership in the thirty-second over. Virgin hoisted Hughes for a particularly satisfying straight six on his way to 53, while Willey hit Lever for three fours in five balls. It was all going swimmingly – at which point 'someone up there' suddenly remembered that Northamptonshire were playing, and the wickets started to fall.

When Sarfraz Nawaz – 'my knees were trembling' – joined George Sharp at 182 for six, the county still needed 14 to win in less than four overs. To the delight of the 4,000 Northamptonshire supporters at HQ, Sharp scored ten of them (a feat which, he later claimed, had aged him at the rate of a year per run) and the target was reached with eleven balls to spare. The duck had been broken. Second place in the Championship, only 16 points behind Mike Brearley's Middlesex, made it the most successful summer in Northamptonshire's history, before or since. The civic reception, plans for which were shelved in 1965, could finally take place.

There might even be some more good news. 'The county's season of success should be further enriched with the name of Peter Willey appearing in the M.C.C. party for India,' enthused the *Northamptonshire Evening Telegraph*. He wasn't picked, proving (as if Northamptonshire needed proof after so many years of trial and tribulation) that you can't win them all.

George Sharp.

Lancashire won the toss and elected to bat

Umpires: HD Bird & AE Fagg

LANCASHIRE

B Wood	retired hurt	14
FM Engineer+	b Dye	0
H Pilling	c Cook b Sarfraz	3
FC Hayes	c&b Hodgson	19
D Lloyd*	b Bedi	48
J Abrahams	b Bedi	46
DP Hughes	not out	39
J Simmons	b Sarfraz	1
RM Ratcliffe	c Larkins b Bedi	4
P Lever	not out	8
PG Lee		
Extras	(b1 lb9 w2 nb1)	13
TOTAL	(7 wkts)	195

FOW: 0,17,45,140,143,148,157

Bowling: Sarfraz 12-2-39-2 Dye 7-3-9-1 Hodgson 6-3-10-1 Larkins 12-4-31-0 Willey 12-2-41-0 Bedi 11-0-52-3

NORTHAMPTONSHIRE

RT Virgin	c&b Ratcliffe	53
P Willey	c Engineer b Lee	65
Mushtaq Mohammad	c Hayes b Ratcliffe	13
DS Steele	c sub b Hughes	24
W Larkins	lbw b Lever	8
G Cook	c Engineer b Lee	15
G Sharp+	not out	10
Sarfraz Nawaz	not out	3
A Hodgson		
BS Bedi		
JCJ Dye		
Extras	(b5 lb1 nb2)	8
TOTAL	(6 wkts)	199

FOW: 103,127,143,154,178,182

Bowling: Lever 12-3-29-1 Lee 12-4-29-2 Simmons 11.1-2-29-0 Ratcliffe 12-2-48-2 Hughes 11-0-56-1

NORTHAMPTONSHIRE WON BY 4 WICKETS

Sussex

22 August 1979 at Hove

Having disposed of the reigning Gillette Cup champions at Lord's in 1976, Northamptonshire were faced with the same task in order to make the final again three years later. Sussex had beaten Somerset to lift the silverware in 1978, and the same two teams were favourites to return to St John's Wood the following season. The semi-finals matched Sussex with Northamptonshire at Hove, while Somerset travelled to face Middlesex.

Much had happened at Wantage Road since Mushtaq Mohammad lifted the trophy on that unforgettable late-summer evening. His own days at the club ended unhappily in the wake of the Kerry Packer affair in 1977; the likes of David Steele, Roy Virgin, Bishan Bedi and John Dye had gone too; Jim Watts was back as captain; and the side contained several new faces, including South African-born Allan Lamb. Northamptonshire had entered the era of the 'Famous Five' – Geoff Cook, Wayne Larkins, Richard Williams, Lamb and Peter Willey – at the top of their order, and runs were rarely in short supply. Bowling sides out was proving an altogether thornier problem.

As it turned out, though, batting setbacks left the county in trouble early on. Cook failed against Geoff Arnold, and Larkins – having opted to continue after a blow on the hand from Imran Khan that broke his little finger – fell victim to Paul Parker's brilliance in the covers as he attempted a sharp single. Williams and Lamb concentrated on repairing the damage, adding 61 in 19 overs, and it was only when Willey joined Lamb that Northamptonshire were really able to wrest the initiative. They put on 157 for the fourth wicket in 32 overs together, Lamb hammering eleven fours in his century and Willey finding the boundary ten times as Arnold Long and his bowlers began to run out of ideas.

Jim Griffiths then rocked Sussex with the wicket of John Barclay, caught behind down the leg side, and despite a brief flourish from Kepler Wessels and Gehan Mendis, who blazed 41 at a rate of six an over, the county reasserted control thanks to Tim Lamb's four-wicket haul and accurate spells from Willey and Watts. The latter, still a formidable competitor at 37, accounted for Imran, while Willey's spectacular diving return catch to remove Peter Graves clinched the Man of the Match award from Ken Barrington. Sussex did not relinquish their grip on the Gillette Cup without a fight, but relinquish it they did, and Northamptonshire's travelling fans headed home to secure their tickets for the final at £6.35 a time.

Somerset cruised through the other semi-final comfortably enough and, a fortnight later, resigned their membership of the trophy-less society with a 45-run victory over one of their long-time partners in adversity. Good for the game, and all that – but wouldn't it have been nice for Jim Watts, that most loyal of county servants, to win something with Northamptonshire before he retired?

Peter Willey.

Northamptonshire won the toss and elected to bat

Umpires: WE Alley & DGL Evans

NORTHAMPTONSHIRE

G Cook	c Long b Arnold	5
W Larkins	run out	11
RG Williams	b Spencer	16
AJ Lamb	c Pigott b Arnold	101
P Willey	b Arnold	89
TJ Yardley	c Spencer b Phillipson	7
G Sharp+	run out	4
PJ Watts*	not out	8
A Hodgson		
TM Lamb		
BJ Griffiths		
Extras	(b9 nb5)	14
TOTAL	(7 wkts)	255

FOW: 13,16,77,234,234,241,255

Bowling: Imran 12-1-55-0 Arnold 12-2-45-3 Pigott 6-0-39-0 Spencer 12-2-34-1 Phillipson 6-1-27-1 Barclay 12-0-41-0

SUSSEX

JRT Barclay	c Sharp b Griffiths	2
KC Wessels	c Sharp b TM Lamb	28
GD Mendis	lbw b Hodgson	69
PWG Parker	lbw b TM Lamb	2
Imran Khan	c Sharp b Watts	11
PJ Graves	c&b Willey	21
CP Phillipson	run out	0
ACS Pigott	lbw b TM Lamb	30
A Long*+	b TM Lamb	15
GG Arnold	not out	18
J Spencer	lbw b Hodgson	6
Extras	(lb11 w2 nb3)	16
TOTAL		218

FOW: 11,45,56,85,138,138,146,185,201

Bowling: Griffiths 10-0-48-1 Hodgson 9.2-0-37-2 TM Lamb 12-2-52-4 Watts 12-1-33-1 Willey 12-2-32-1

NORTHAMPTONSHIRE WON BY 37 RUNS

ESSEX

21 July 1980 at Lord's

'Of all the Lord's cup finals of the past eighteen years,' wrote Michael Melford in the *Daily Telegraph*, 'none has had a more remarkable last hour than the Benson & Hedges final which Northamptonshire won yesterday evening by six runs.' It was equally true that never in the county's history had a captain deserved his moment of triumph more than Jim Watts, whose shrewd generalship and faithfulness to the cause were at long last rewarded with a trophy in his hands.

Getting his side to the final had been a notable achievement in itself. The semi-final, away to Middlesex, was an enthralling affair; Northamptonshire 206 for seven, the home side 128 for five from 41 overs at the end of a rain-shortened day, with Mike Gatting unbeaten on 59 and apparently holding the key to the match. Next morning, Watts manipulated his attack cleverly. He persisted with the spinners, even when Gatting and Vintcent Van der Bijl looked to have their measure, and Peter Willey eventually removed the big South African before Sarfraz Nawaz returned with three wickets in seven balls to win the game.

The final was only marginally less gripping. Heavy rain ruled out any play on the Saturday, triggering an epidemic of 24-hour stomach bugs throughout Northamptonshire which enabled the individuals thus afflicted to return to Lord's on Monday morning. Allan Lamb held the county's innings together with 72, and his seventh-wicket partnership of 59 in ten overs with Watts helped to ease the total past 200. But Essex were into their stride quickly; they sauntered to 112 for one

Nearly there! Sarfraz Nawaz bowls Neil Smith and Northamptonshire scent victory.

Northamptonshire, under Jim Watts, celebrate their 1980 Benson & Hedges Cup triumph.

and, with Graham Gooch and Ken McEwan at the crease, needed only 98 from 22 overs.

It was Tim Lamb who broke through, inducing a loose drive from Gooch. Then McEwan played on attempting to cut Willey, Watts removed Brian Hardie for a duck and Keith Pont fell prey to Richard Williams' flighted off-spin. It was 129 for five, and Northamptonshire were back on top, thanks largely to their two slow men, who between them sent down 18 successive overs from the Nursery End at a cost of only 53.

However, there simply had to be a sting in the tail. Norbert Phillip provided it by smashing 30 off two overs from Jim Griffiths, and the contest came down to the last over – bowled by Sarfraz – from which a dozen runs were needed. Neil Smith's stumps were rattled by the second ball, Ray East nipped a single from the third, and the task of scoring ten from the final three deliveries proved beyond even the hard-hitting Phillip. Northamptonshire had their second one-day title, four years after the first.

Lamb claimed the Gold Award and Watts took possession of the Benson & Hedges Cup. He then calmly announced his retirement from the first-class game at the end of the season. Watts' timing could not be faulted, and neither could his contribution to Northamptonshire cricket.

Richard Williams.

Northamptonshire won the toss and elected to bat

Umpires: DJ Constant & BJ Meyer

NORTHAMPTONSHIRE

G Cook	c Gooch b Pont	29
W Larkins	c Denness b Pont	18
RG Williams	c McEwan b Pont	15
AJ Lamb	c Hardie b Phillip	72
P Willey	c McEwan b Turner	15
TJ Yardley	c Smith b Gooch	0
G Sharp+	c Fletcher b Pont	8
PJ Watts*	run out	22
Sarfraz Nawaz	not out	10
TM Lamb	lbw b Turner	4
BJ Griffiths	b Turner	0
Extras	(b1 lb8 w4 nb3)	16
TOTAL		209

FOW: 36,61,78,110,110,132,190,193,209

Bowling: Lever 11-3-38-0 Phillip 11-1-38-1 Turner 10.5-2-33-3 Pont 11-1-60-4
Gooch 11-0-24-1

ESSEX

MH Denness	b Willey	14
GA Gooch	c AJ Lamb b TM Lamb	60
KS McEwan	b Willey	38
KWR Fletcher*	b Sarfraz	29
BR Hardie	b Watts	0
KR Pont	b Williams	2
S Turner	c Watts b Sarfraz	16
N Phillip	not out	32
N Smith+	b Sarfraz	2
RE East	not out	1
JK Lever		
Extras	(b1 lb5 w3)	9
TOTAL	(8 wkts)	203

FOW: 52,112,118,121,129,160,180,198

Bowling: Sarfraz 11-3-23-3 Griffiths 7-0-46-0 Watts 8-1-30-1 TM Lamb 11-0-42-1
Willey 11-1-34-2 Williams 7-0-19-1

NORTHAMPTONSHIRE WON BY 6 RUNS

LANCASHIRE

19 August 1981 at Northampton

In 1921, Northamptonshire lost to Warwick Armstrong's mighty Australians by an innings and 484 runs, and *Wisden* felt it 'ludicrous' that the teams should have met on equal terms. On the face of it, the individual contest between Michael Holding with the ball and Jim Griffiths with the bat on a gloomy August evening six decades later was equally preposterous. Just a few months earlier, in Barbados, 'Whispering Death' had delivered one of the swiftest overs in Test history to Geoff Boycott who did well to get nought. That was an experience only too familiar to Griffiths; he failed to score in 51 of his 138 first-class innings and 'boasted' a career average of 3.33. And yet there he stood, partnered by fellow tail-ender Tim Lamb, trying to scrape together the handful of runs necessary to carry Northamptonshire into the first NatWest Trophy final.

Lancashire's modest total appeared to justify Geoff Cook's decision to bowl first on winning the toss. The visitors were well-placed at 116 for one just past the halfway mark, but once Richard Williams had broken the century partnership between Graeme Fowler and David Lloyd, the innings fell away. George Sharp's superb diving catch, at full stretch down the leg side, accounted for Clive Lloyd off Lamb, and the future ECB chief executive also removed Bernard Reidy and John Abrahams as Lancashire lost eight wickets for 45. Holding helped Jack Simmons put on 25 handy runs at the end, but Northamptonshire still fancied their chances, particularly at 96 for two in reply with Williams and Allan Lamb at the crease. Then 'Flat Jack' sent them both back to the pavilion; the picture altogether less rosy at 97 for four. The fascinating ebb and flow continued, with Jim Yardley and Bob Carter – now Northamptonshire's director of cricket, then a slightly nervous twenty-one-year-old deputising for the injured Peter Willey – adding 53, before Reidy's left-arm seam put Lancashire back on top. The last pair came together at 174 for nine with eight overs remaining, and Griffiths walked to the middle in decidedly unfriendly light to face a decidedly unfriendly bowler.

Crisis? What crisis? 'Big Jim' dug out a Holding yorker with aplomb – the moment at which 'Tiger Tim' began to feel it might still be Northamptonshire's day. In nervy ones and twos the scores were brought level, and as the last over beckoned, the two batsmen consulted with umpires Lloyd Budd and Alan Whitehead. If the teams finished equal on runs and wickets, the deciding factor would be the score after 30 overs. The two officials confirmed that the home side had the edge; a maiden would do it, assuming the final wicket remained intact. And the good news was that Holding had bowled out his 12-over allocation. David Lloyd, slow left-arm, sent down three 'dot' balls to Griffiths. The fourth drew a big appeal for a bat-pad catch, rejected by Budd; the fifth turned, scuttled past wicketkeeper Fowler and the two heroes completed a match-winning bye. Illogical, captain.

The pride of Irthlingborough was chaired off the field by a few of the 7,000 spectators present, and proceeded to give a memorable television interview to Richie Benaud. Lamb, three for 28 and an undefeated 10, earned the Man of the Match award from Jim Parks. Only one negative thought tempered the general euphoria; the final could only be an anti-climax.

Man of the Match Tim Lamb – crucial wickets and decisive runs.

Lancashire v. Northamptonshire

Northamptonshire won the toss and elected to field

Umpires: WL Budd & AGT Whitehead

LANCASHIRE

A Kennedy	c Yardley b Sarfraz	6
G Fowler+	c Sharp b Williams	57
D Lloyd	c Carter b Williams	52
CH Lloyd*	c Sharp b TM Lamb	4
DP Hughes	c TM Lamb b Sarfraz	13
BW Reidy	lbw b TM Lamb	0
J Abrahams	c Sharp b TM Lamb	2
J Simmons	not out	28
SJ O'Shaughnessy	b Griffiths	3
PJW Allott	lbw b Griffiths	0
MA Holding	not out	12
Extras	(lb7 w1 nb1)	9
TOTAL	(9 wkts)	186

FOW: 6,116,123,123,123,133,144,160,161

Bowling 1st: Sarfraz 12-2-35-2 Griffiths 12-1-46-2 Mallender 12-3-28-0 TM Lamb 12-1-28-3 Williams 12-0-40-2

NORTHAMPTONSHIRE

G Cook*	b O'Shaughnessy	31
W Larkins	lbw b Allott	9
RG Williams	c CH Lloyd b Simmons	41
AJ Lamb	c D Lloyd b Simmons	10
TJ Yardley	c CH Lloyd b Reidy	31
RM Carter	lbw b D Lloyd	14
G Sharp+	lbw b Reidy	1
Sarfraz Nawaz	lbw b Reidy	14
NA Mallender	c Fowler b Allott	4
TM Lamb	not out	10
BJ Griffiths	not out	1
Extras	(b2 lb16 w1 nb2)	21
TOTAL	(9 wkts)	187

FOW: 24,58,96,97,150,152,162,170,174

Bowling: Holding 12-2-36-0 Allott 12-2-32-2 O'Shaughnessy 4-0-25-1 Reidy 10-3-22-3 Simmons 12-4-17-2 D Lloyd 9.5-0-34-1

NORTHAMPTONSHIRE WON BY 1 WICKET

DERBYSHIRE

5 September 1981 at Lord's

The day after Northamptonshire's heart-stopping victory over Lancashire at Wantage Road, Derbyshire won the other semi-final in equally hectic circumstances. They tied with Essex at Derby, and progressed by virtue of losing only eight wickets to their opponents' ten, with Bob Taylor and Paul Newman haring through for the decisive single off the very last ball. 'Anyone who thinks (the final) is going to be drab and uninteresting because two so-called unfashionable teams are involved, couldn't be more wrong,' observed county skipper Geoff Cook, looking to win a trophy in his first full season at the helm. Not drab and uninteresting, maybe, but surely the summer had already used up its quota of breathtaking excitement? Headingley '81 and all that. Cook and Wayne Larkins – both regarded as 'possibles' for England's forthcoming tour to India – launched Northamptonshire's innings in sound rather than spectacular fashion, posting 99 in 29 overs before Geoff Miller ended Larkins' stay with a well-judged catch just inside the ropes at deep midwicket. Allan Lamb, the batting linchpin in Northamptonshire's Lord's triumph against Essex fourteen months earlier, missed out this time, and it soon became a matter of who, if anyone, would stay with captain Cook.

Ten years on from his county debut, Cook batted with authority and flair on the way to 111 from 144 balls with eleven fours. Apart from his opening partner, no one else reached 20. Derbyshire's fielding, with Barry Wood leading by example, was every bit as outstanding as the loss of Lamb, Peter Willey and Jim Yardley to run-outs might suggest. At 204 for three, Northamptonshire had been counting on something very much more formidable than 235 for nine, and they might have notched a few more but for Cook's dismissal to a leg-before decision that doesn't look a great deal more convincing now than it did in 1981.

A couple of hours later, he faced the task of lifting his side, with Derbyshire at 164 for one, courtesy of a 123-run stand between John Wright and Peter Kirsten. Neil Mallender, the twenty-year-old Yorkshire-born paceman who had bowled so tidily in the semi, gave Northamptonshire hope by trapping both partners in front, and further timely successes – including the wicket of David Steele, who would return to Wantage Road the following season – pushed the requirement up to 19 from the last two overs. Colin Tunnicliffe then clubbed two boundaries off Sarfraz Nawaz, and Derbyshire needed seven runs from the final over, to be bowled by the star of seventeen days earlier, Jim Griffiths. Once again, however, wickets were an issue; six runs would suffice, barring a major collapse. Tunnicliffe and Miller scored five off as many balls, and after a long delay as Cook sorted out his field, they scampered home for a leg-bye in a near-identical copy of their semi-final victory.

'I'd rather have got a duck and won the damned game,' said Cook, after collecting two medals – one as Man of the Match, the other, less welcome, as a loser. A couple of days later, his name appeared in England's winter tour party; while that of Larkins did not, prompting his decision to join the 'rebel' trip to South Africa. If Miller had muffed that catch on the boundary – who knows?

The 'nearly' men – Northamptonshire's side in the 1981 NatWest Trophy Final. From left to right, standing: R.G. Williams, W. Larkins, T.J. Yardley, T.M. Lamb, B.J. Griffiths, N.A. Mallender. Seated: A.J. Lamb, P. Willey, G. Cook (captain), G. Sharp, Sarfraz Nawaz.

Derbyshire won the toss and elected to field

Umpires: DJ Constant & KE Palmer

NORTHAMPTONSHIRE

G Cook*	lbw b Tunnicliffe	111
W Larkins	c Miller b Wood	52
AJ Lamb	run out	9
RG Williams	c Hill b Miller	14
P Willey	run out	19
TJ Yardley	run out	4
G Sharp+	c Kirsten b Tunnicliffe	5
Sarfraz Nawaz	not out	3
NA Mallender	c Taylor b Newman	0
TM Lamb	b Hendrick	4
BJ Griffiths		
Extras	(b2 lb9 w1 nb2)	14
TOTAL	(9 wkts)	235

FOW: 99,137,168,204,218,225,227,227,235

Bowling: Hendrick 12-3-50-1 Tunnicliffe 12-1-42-2 Wood 12-2-35-1 Newman 12-0-37-1 Steele 5-0-31-0 Miller 7-0-26-1

DERBYSHIRE

A Hill	b Mallender	14
JG Wright	lbw b Mallender	76
PN Kirsten	lbw b Mallender	63
B Wood*	b Sarfraz	10
KJ Barnett	run out	19
DS Steele	b Griffiths	0
G Miller	not out	22
CJ Tunnicliffe	not out	15
RW Taylor+		
PG Newman		
M Hendrick		
Extras	(b5 lb7 w3 nb1)	16
TOTAL	(6 wkts)	235

FOW: 41,164,165,189,191,213

Bowling: Sarfraz 12-2-58-1 Griffiths 12-2-40-1 Mallender 10-1-35-3 Willey 12-0-33-0 TM Lamb 12-0-43-0 Williams 2-0-10-0

DERBYSHIRE WON ON FEWER WICKETS LOST

DERBYSHIRE

14, 16, 17 August 1982 at Northampton

They appeared to have very little in common; the ebullient 'Haryana Hurricane', well on the way to becoming a national hero and one of Test cricket's most prolific all-rounders, and the richly-talented but somewhat diffident Cambridge blue, who turned his back on the professional game at the age of twenty-eight. But Kapil Dev and Robin Boyd-Moss joined forces to give supporters at Wantage Road one of the most entertaining batting displays seen on the ground for many years.

Boyd-Moss, a product of Bedford School who represented his university at rugby union as well as cricket, hit 3 sixes and 18 fours in his majestic 137 in the first innings, adding 170 for the fourth wicket with Richard Williams after Wayne Larkins had set the tone with his fifth century of the summer. Then the Indian star inflicted further punishment on Derbyshire's bowlers, blazing a 30-ball half-century to hasten Geoff Cook's declaration. Before the close, the visitors lost their captain, Barry Wood, caught by Boyd-Moss at mid-on. It had been very much his day.

John Wright dominated proceedings on the Monday, underlining his liking for the Northamptonshire attack. At Derby a few weeks earlier, his unbeaten 185 had secured a seven-wicket victory for his side; now he followed up with 157, featuring 23 boundaries. The county led by 125, but lost four wickets for 46 in a disastrous session after tea which brought Derbyshire right back into the match with a day to go. Much then depended on Boyd-Moss and Kapil, and their decision to launch a counter-attack paid off handsomely.

Paul Newman was off the field, nursing a groin injury, but Derbyshire still had seamers Steve Oldham and Colin Tunnicliffe and their towering left-arm spinner Dallas Moir, all perfectly competent professionals. They might as well have been bowling underarm in the back garden. Northamptonshire's fifth-wicket pair unleashed a barrage of thrilling strokes, putting on 182 in just over an hour-and-a-half; their stand went from 50 to 100 inside four overs, with Boyd-Moss on-driving Oldham for four successive boundaries. Kapil, who had plundered 75 from 48 deliveries in a John Player League game against the same opponents at Bletchley a couple of days earlier, played every shot in the book, and one or two that weren't. Like a boxing referee stepping in to save a reeling fighter from unnecessary punishment, Cook called a halt and left Derbyshire to score 354 for victory in four-and-a-quarter hours.

Still a little shell-shocked, they struggled to 64 for four at tea. Then Neil Mallender went to work with a burst of five wickets in 17 balls after the break, and Northamptonshire were home and dry after a performance in all departments that illuminated an otherwise pretty lack-lustre season.

Robin Boyd-Moss receives the 'Young Batsman of the Year' award from Ted Dexter in 1982 – but county cricket saw the last of him just five years later.

Northamptonshire won the toss and elected to bat

Umpires: AGT Whitehead & R Julian

NORTHAMPTONSHIRE

G Cook*	c&b Moir	20	c Maher b Newman		1
W Larkins	c Moir b Wood	105	c Anderson b Tunnicliffe		29
P Willey	c Tunnicliffe b Moir	0	c&b Tunnicliffe		7
RJ Boyd-Moss	c Oldham b Moir	137	not out		80
RG Williams	c Moir b Tunnicliffe	58	c sub b Moir		4
Kapil Dev	not out	65	not out		100
DS Steele	not out	3			
DJ Wild					
G Sharp+					
NA Mallender					
BJ Griffiths					
Extras	(lb6 nb6)	12	(lb1 nb6)		7
TOTAL	(5 wkts dec)	400	(4 wkts dec)		228

FOW 1st: 78,78,155,325,377
FOW 2nd: 1,35,39,46

Bowling 1st: Oldham 15-2-59-0 Tunnicliffe 19.2-2-95-1 Newman 13-2-50-0 Wood 23-3-78-1 Moir 34-9-106-3

Bowling 2nd: Oldham 12-2-79-0 Newman 5-0-23-1 Tunnicliffe 12-1-53-2 Moir 16.3-3-66-1

DERBYSHIRE

B Wood*	c Boyd-Moss b Mallender	3		c Kapil Dev b Mallender	42
JG Wright	b Mallender	157		c Sharp b Mallender	20
PN Kirsten	st Sharp b Steele	48		c Kapil Dev b Mallender	5
KJ Barnett	c Cook b Willey	46		lbw b Williams	12
IS Anderson	b Willey	0		lbw b Griffiths	5
CJ Tunnicliffe	not out	13	(7)	c Boyd-Moss b Mallender	6
PG Newman	c Steele b Mallender	0	(8)	b Kapil Dev	14
BJM Maher+	not out	4	(10)	c Steele b Mallender	0
JH Hampshire			(6)	not out	6
DG Moir			(9)	c Kapil Dev b Mallender	0
S Oldham				lbw b Mallender	0
Extras	(b1 lb2 nb1)	4		(lb6 nb1)	7
TOTAL	(6 wkts dec)	275			117

FOW 1st: 3,101,240,240,266,266
FOW 2nd: 28,34,54,67,93,99,99,103,103

Bowling 1st: Kapil Dev 18-5-33-0 Mallender 16-2-55-3 Willey 8-1-21-2 Griffiths 12-0-53-0 Steele 31-14-55-1 Williams 15-3-54-0

Bowling 2nd: Kapil Dev 14.2-532-1 Mallender 19-9-41-7 Willey 7-4-8-0 Steele 8-4-13-0 Griffiths 4-2-2-1 Williams 6-1-14-1

NORTHAMPTONSHIRE WON BY 236 RUNS

SURREY

Despite their successes in the longer one-day games during the 1980s, Northamptonshire remained a maddeningly inconsistent side on Sunday afternoons. Occasionally brilliant, especially when one or more of their 'Famous Five' batsmen fired on all cylinders, they could also plumb the depths. Rather like Longfellow's little girl with the curl – when they were good they were very, very good, but when they were bad they were horrid.

The arrival of Roger Harper in 1985 livened up Northamptonshire's out-cricket enormously, and they mounted a serious challenge for the John Player League title that summer. But their quest for 40-over honours hit trouble in August with three matches in a row – against Nottinghamshire, Somerset and Glamorgan – rained off. Fortunately, the weather improved for the trip to Woodbridge Road, and the county, as joint-leaders, needed to take full advantage.

Rob Bailey, in his second season as a first-team regular, shared an opening stand of 56 with Wayne Larkins, but at the halfway stage of the innings Northamptonshire only had 89 on the board. Acceleration was clearly the order of the day, and the county scene had few players better equipped to provide it than Larkins and Allan Lamb. Surrey's bowling was below strength and the pair piled on 232 in 34 overs together, with Larkins progressing from 50 to 126 in just 40 balls, including 8 sixes. Lamb was also at his bullying best, powering to 132 not out from 85 deliveries with 4 sixes – one of them off the last ball of the innings – and 14 fours. It was then, and remains going into the 2002 season, Northamptonshire's highest total in the competition.

The early loss of Alan Butcher and Graham Clinton made Surrey's already daunting task even more difficult, but Monte Lynch set about the county attack with great gusto and raced to his half-century in 32 balls before Harper caught him on the boundary off Duncan Wild, as he attempted to clear the ropes for the fifth time. Was Harper inside the line when he held the ball? Some Surrey supporters had their doubts; but the spectators nearest the incident had made

the journey down from Northamptonshire and were all, apparently, quite satisfied that Law 32.2 had not been transgressed.

Andy Needham offered some further resistance but Surrey fell a long way short of their target, and victory the following Sunday at Headingley sent Northamptonshire to Worcester on the final day of the season with still a sniff of the title. They duly lost at New Road in a rain-affected game; Essex, Sussex, Hampshire and Derbyshire all won, and Geoff Cook's side had to settle for fifth place. The prize money, needless to say, only went down to fourth.

Wayne Larkins.

Surrey won the toss and elected to field

Umpires: JH Hampshire & AA Jones

NORTHAMPTONSHIRE

W Larkins	c Ward b Feltham	126
RJ Bailey	lbw b Pauline	21
AJ Lamb	not out	132
RA Harper	not out	13
RJ Boyd-Moss		
RG Williams		
DJ Wild		
G Cook*		
D Ripley+		
NA Mallender		
A Walker		
Extras	(b4 lb7 w3)	14
TOTAL	(2 wkts)	306

FOW: 56,232

Bowling: Waterman 8-1-46-0 Doughty 8-0-46-0 Feltham 8-0-72-1 Pauline 8-0-53-1 Needham 4-0-33-0 Butcher 4-0-45-0

SURREY

AR Butcher*	c Ripley b Walker	9
GS Clinton	b Mallender	13
MA Lynch	c Harper b Wild	55
AJ Stewart+	b Harper	11
A Needham	run out	51
DM Ward	c Cook b Harper	9
RJ Doughty	c Walker b Wild	10
MA Feltham	b Walker	31
DB Pauline	c Wild b Williams	3
CK Bullen	c Wild b Williams	9
PA Waterman	not out	0
Extras	(lb9 w2 nb1)	12
TOTAL		213

FOW: 21,29,96,104,132,155,183,197,212

Bowling: Mallender 5-0-19-1 Walker 6.1-0-26-0 Harper 8-0-40-2 Larkins 3-0-39-0 Wild 8-0-44-2 Williams 5-0-36-2

NORTHAMPTONSHIRE WON BY 93 RUNS

SUSSEX

28, 30 June, 1 July 1986 at Hastings

Few cricket enthusiasts with memories of the old Central Ground in Hastings can visit the shopping centre that now occupies the site without feeling sorrow and anger in roughly equal measure. However well-appointed the town's new ground may be, it will never match the old one for charm – surrounded by tall, stern-faced houses, overlooked by the ruined castle, the smells of ozone and seaside hotel 'evening meals' assailing the nostrils. Its disappearance under concrete hurt, as the historian Gerald Brodribb noted, 'like the loss of a dear friend'.

The last of Northamptonshire's eight Championship visits there, in 1986, was indeed a classic match. If there was one sight more exhilarating for county followers than Allan Lamb in full flow, it was an *irritated* Allan Lamb in full flow. Being left out of the England team for the Third Test against India at Edgbaston inspired Lamb to produce one of the best of his many match-winning innings for the club. Ironically, Wayne Larkins was recalled by the selectors for the same game while in some of the worst form of his career, but never made it to Birmingham.

The two spinners, acting-captain Roger Harper and Nick Cook (in his first year with Northamptonshire after crossing the great divide from Grace Road), got through most of the work on the opening day, but it was the Sussex seamers who proved destructive on the second. Imran Khan, Tony Pigott, Dermot Reeve and Colin Wells shared the wickets, and it took some tail-end defiance from Cook and Neil Mallender to save the follow-on. Imran and Paul Parker then built briskly on the home side's first innings lead of 147, and Ian Gould declared before the start of the final day's play to leave Northamptonshire needing 321 for an unlikely win.

Unlikely at the start, and even more so as Larkins failed to keep down a lifting ball from

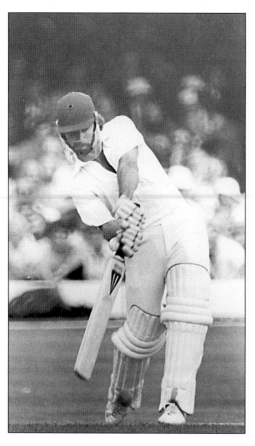

Pigott that not only dismissed him but chipped a bone in his hand, ruling him out of the Test. When Imran bowled Robin Boyd-Moss, the county had lost two good wickets for a single on a pitch described by *Wisden* as 'of dubious character' and by Lamb, who joined makeshift opener David Capel in a bid to stop the rot, as 'a bloody minefield.' It amounted to the same thing.

Against all the odds, the pair put on 172 for the third wicket. Lamb, in 'Fighting Temeraire' mode, then added a further 87 with Rob Bailey, and went on to a magnificent 157 off 153 balls with 27 fours. But Sussex weren't finished and reduced Northamptonshire from 282 for four to 301 for nine; meaning that a further 20 runs were required from the last pair, Mallender and Alan Walker. By this stage, batting was a far from pleasant pastime as the track deteriorated, but the two Yorkshiremen proved equal to the task. Walker drove Imran for the winning run to end a superb game – the memory of which, happily, did not disappear with the venue.

Allan Lamb – one of many extraordinary innings from the South African-born star.

Sussex won the toss and elected to bat

Umpires: AA Jones & R Julian

SUSSEX

DK Standing	c Cook b Harper	22	c Harper b Capel	16
AM Green	b Harper	55	lbw b Capel	28
PWG Parker	c&b Cook	26	b Wild	54
Imran Khan	c Waterton b Capel	59	not out	62
CM Wells	c Lamb b Harper	11	not out	12
AP Wells	lbw b Capel	44		
RI Alikhan	not out	27		
IJ Gould*+	b Cook	1		
DA Reeve	c Walker b Cook	10		
ACS Pigott	c Boyd-Moss b Mallender	10		
AM Bredin				
Extras	(b8 lb5 nb5)	18	(lb1)	1
TOTAL	(9 wkts dec)	283	(3 wkts dec)	173

FOW 1st: 72,83,133,148,232,235,236,258,283
FOW 2nd: 43,52,146

Bowling 1st: Mallender 13.5-3-28-1 Walker 11-2-37-0 Capel 12-0-30-2 Harper 29-8-79-3 Cook 34-11-72-3 Boyd-Moss 4-1-14-0 Wild 3-0-10-0

Bowling 2nd: Mallender 12-5-26-0 Walker 13-4-42-0 Capel 12-0-48-2 Harper 5-1-9-0 Cook 16-6-30-0 Wild 6-0-17-1

NORTHAMPTONSHIRE

DJ Capel	c Parker b Pigott	13	b Imran	54
W Larkins	c Gould b Imran	9	c CM Wells b Pigott	0
RJ Boyd-Moss	c Gould b CM Wells	17	b Imran	0
AJ Lamb	c Standing b Imran	20	c sub b Pigott	157
RJ Bailey	c Alikhan b Reeve	7	c Gould b CM Wells	57
DJ Wild	lbw b Reeve	0	c Reeve b CM Wells	18
RA Harper*	lbw b CM Wells	22	lbw b CM Wells	0
SNV Waterton+	lbw b CM Wells	9	run out	3
NGB Cook	b Imran	18	b CM Wells	1
NA Mallender	not out	7	not out	8
A Walker	c Standing b CM Wells	1	not out	13
Extras	(b3 lb7 nb3)	13	(b1 lb6 nb3)	10
TOTAL		136	(9 wkts)	321

FOW 1st: 25,25,46,57,57,94,99,111,135
FOW 2nd: 0,1,173,260,282,282,285,288,301

Bowling 1st: Imran 16-2-44-3 Pigott 9-3-19-1 Reeve 11-5-26-2 Standing 6-1-14-0 CM Wells 7.2-2-23-4

Bowling 2nd: Imran 18.5-1-66-2 Pigott 15-4-61-2 Reeve 10-3-46-0 Standing 8-1-35-0 CM Wells 17-2-72-4 Bredin 6-2-34-0

NORTHAMPTONSHIRE WON BY 1 WICKET

KENT

10 June 1987 at Canterbury

For Northamptonshire's players, officials and supporters, 1987 was the 'Jekyll-and-Hyde' season to end them all. Geoff Cook's side might easily have done the 'treble' of County Championship, NatWest Trophy and Benson & Hedges Cup. In fact, they won nothing – and collected a few scars that took years, rather than weeks or months, to heal. But they played some excellent cricket along the way, not least at the St Lawrence Ground where the Benson & Hedges semi-final against Kent threw up what Man of the Match adjudicator Denis Compton described as 'one of the best limited-overs innings ever.' His task that day was about as straightforward as they come.

The county's bowling generally left a good deal to be desired in the first half of the match, leaving aside tidy spells from Winston Davis and Duncan Wild. Kent's acceleration was provided by Chris Tavare and Chris Cowdrey, whose fourth-wicket stand of 115 occupied only 15 overs. Cowdrey was in particularly aggressive mood, hitting 4 sixes and 5 fours in his 87 from 61 balls. The spinners, Richard Williams and Nick Cook, came in for some particularly harsh treatment.

After losing the vital wicket of Wayne Larkins early in their reply, Northamptonshire struggled to find any momentum and toiled to 89 for three from 29 overs. At that stage, they still needed 187 from 26, and despite a determined stand of 111 between Allan Lamb and David Capel, the target was a daunting 97 off the last ten overs. But Northamptonshire had enjoyed a welcome stroke of good fortune when Eldine Baptiste, a key member of Kent's attack who would spend a season at Wantage Road in 1991, pulled up with a groin strain. Cowdrey needed to 'find' overs from occasional bowlers, and that was all the encouragement Lamb needed.

With Wild as his willing partner, he combined trademark drives and cuts with some frantic running – the pair regularly taking on fielders to turn ones into twos, and twos into threes. They undermined Kent with sheer nerve, and carried Northamptonshire to the threshold of a crowd-silencing victory in increasingly poor light. With the score at 271 and three balls remaining, Lamb straight-drove Chris Penn to the fence and ran from the field to mastermind the celebrations.

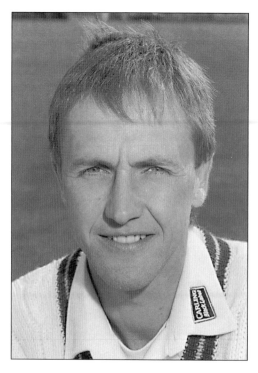

Unfortunately, he had misread the scoreboard and was turned around by his colleagues at the top of the pavilion steps. The next delivery was edged to the boundary and the case of champagne in the visitors' dressing room took an instant and hefty hammering. Lamb's unbeaten 126 came off 101 balls with a six and 10 fours.

But perhaps all the luck had been used up. In the final, Yorkshire won by virtue of losing fewer wickets in a tie. A high-quality Larkins century against Essex followed by an impressive all-round team effort against Leicestershire took Northamptonshire to Lord's again in the NatWest, only for Nottinghamshire, in the shape of Richard Hadlee, to snatch victory in a flurry of boundaries and dropped catches on Blue Monday, after looking dead and buried on Saturday evening. Another classic match? One for the Nottinghamshire collection, possibly.

Duncan Wild – the perfect supporting role.

Northamptonshire won the toss and elected to field

Umpires: JH Hampshire & NT Plews

KENT

MR Benson	b Davis	46
SG Hinks	c Lamb b Capel	7
DG Aslett	b Wild	11
CJ Tavare	b Davis	78
CS Cowdrey*	c G Cook b NGB Cook	87
GR Cowdrey	c Ripley b Davis	9
EAE Baptiste	not out	11
SA Marsh+	c G Cook b NGB Cook	4
C Penn		
DJM Kelleher		
DL Underwood		
Extras	(b1 lb9 w10 nb2)	22
TOTAL	(7 wkts)	275

FOW: 9,53,110,225,239,268,275

Bowling: Davis 11-1-37-3 Capel 11-0-51-1 Walker 10-0-58-0 Wild 11-1-23-1 NGB Cook 10-0-64-2 Williams 2-0-32-0

NORTHAMPTONSHIRE

G Cook*	c GR Cowdrey b Underwood	40
W Larkins	c Marsh b Baptiste	3
RJ Bailey	c Marsh b Penn	29
AJ Lamb	not out	126
DJ Capel	b Kelleher	47
RG Williams	b Underwood	6
DJ Wild	not out	10
D Ripley+		
NGB Cook		
WW Davis		
A Walker		
Extras	(b1 lb7 w10)	18
TOTAL	(5 wkts)	279

FOW: 12,76,89,200,211

Bowling 1st: Baptiste 6-3-8-1 Kelleher 11-0-47-1 Penn 10.4-0-60-1 Underwood 11-0-64-2 CS Cowdrey 9-0-55-0 Hinks 3-0-19-0 GR Cowdrey 4-0-18-0

NORTHAMPTONSHIRE WON BY 5 WICKETS

YORKSHIRE

27, 29, 30 June 1987 at Northampton

More often than not, the loss of an entire day to rain in a three-day match would debase the contest. Not so on this occasion. Richard Blakey for Yorkshire, and Northamptonshire's David Capel and Rob Bailey, all produced performances out of the top drawer, culminating in one of Wantage Road's most stirring finishes of recent times.

The weather ruled out any cricket on Saturday. On Sunday, down at Guildford for a Refuge Assurance League game against Surrey, Capel learned (from a gateman!) of his selection for the Third Test against Pakistan, starting at Headingley later in the week. He would become the first Northampton-born cricketer to play for England since George Thompson made the last of his six Test appearances, against South Africa at Cape Town in March 1910. On the Monday morning, Geoff Cook put Yorkshire in to bat on a green pitch, and Capel handed the press corps a ready-made 'celebrated his call-up' story by claiming seven for 46 – then a career-best. But Blakey deserved a few headlines of his own, stroking 15 fours in a fine century that saved Yorkshire from humiliation; of the other batsmen, only Peter Hartley passed 20.

Cook then raised the stakes. He settled into a familiar secondary role as Wayne Larkins enjoyed himself, hitting 88 of his 101 runs in boundaries, and declared still 49 behind. Yorkshire had increased their lead by 22 without loss at the close, and with his team looking to stay among the Championship pacesetters, Phil Carrick was prepared to make a game of it – although the prospect of a repeat performance from Larkins made him err, not unreasonably, on the side of caution. He set Northamptonshire a target of 283 in an hour-and-three-quarters, plus the last 20 overs – a total of 45 overs, in the event – and watched with relief as Cook and Larkins departed with only nine on the board. Allan Lamb also went cheaply, while Rob Bailey was hit in the face by a ball from Hartley. He batted on in some discomfort.

Very soon, however, it was Bailey's turn to inflict pain. He and Capel fired off boundary after boundary in a dazzling stand worth 208 off 165 balls, Bailey issuing the clearest possible statement of intent by thumping Hartley onto the football pitch. It was one of 4 sixes, plus 18 fours, in his 128-ball blast, while Capel faced 85 deliveries and reached the fence eleven times. Northamptonshire breezed home with nine balls to spare, climbing to third place in the table, and the club's idiosyncratic but much-loved public address announcer, 'Rambling Ron' Staniford, suggested that everyone should stand as the two batsmen walked off the field. In truth, no one needed to be told to do it.

Rob Bailey.

Northamptonshire won the toss and elected to field

Umpires: R Julian & KJ Lyons

YORKSHIRE

MD Moxon	c Lamb b Capel	1	c Ripley b Capel		12
AA Metcalfe	c Ripley b Capel	0	c Davis b NGB Cook		26
RJ Blakey	c Ripley b Capel	108	b NGB Cook		60
K Sharp	c Wild b Davis	0	st Ripley b Williams		49
JD Love	c Larkins b Davis	7	not out		48
DL Bairstow+	c Walker b Capel	15			
P Carrick*	c Ripley b Capel	2	not out		22
A Sidebottom	lbw b Walker	1	(6) c Larkins b Williams		3
PJ Hartley	c Davis b Capel	23			
PW Jarvis	c Ripley b Capel	3			
SD Fletcher	not out	1			
Extras	(b3 lb4 w10 nb9)	26	(b1 lb10 w1 nb1)		13
TOTAL		187	(5 wkts dec)		233

FOW 1st: 0,1,6,30,90,97,98,178,186
FOW 2nd: 37,67,154,169,185

Bowling 1st: Capel 18.2-3-46-7 Davis 21-4-73-2 Walker 15-5-51-1 NGB Cook 9-6-10-0

Bowling 2nd: Capel 10-7-10-1 Davis 10-2-24-0 Walker 11-1-35-0 NGB Cook 21-3-48-2 Wild 7-1-35-0 Williams 11-3-29-2 G Cook 7-2-41-0

NORTHAMPTONSHIRE

G Cook*	not out	31	b Sidebottom		7
W Larkins	not out	101	lbw b Jarvis		2
RJ Bailey			not out		152
AJ Lamb			c&b Fletcher		14
DJ Capel			not out		91
RG Williams					
DJ Wild					
D Ripley+					
NGB Cook					
WW Davis					
A Walker					
Extras	(b4 lb1 nb1)	6	(b1 lb16)		17
TOTAL	(0 wkt dec)	138	(3 wkts)		283

FOW 1st: -
FOW 2nd: 9,9,75

Bowling 1st: Jarvis 8-1-53-0 Sidebottom 10-4-25-0 Hartley 6-1-32-0 Fletcher 6-2-22-0 Carrick 1-0-1-0

Bowling 2nd: Jarvis 14-2-85-1 Sidebottom 11.3-0-66-1 Hartley 8-0-57-0 Fletcher 8-1-42-1 Carrick 2-0-16-0

NORTHAMPTONSHIRE WON BY 7 WICKETS

WARWICKSHIRE

17, 18, 19, 20 May 1988 at Northampton

Opinion was sharply divided over the desirability of four-day matches in the County Championship, introduced in 1988. Many feared that Parkinson's Law would inevitably apply; work expanding to fill the time available, making the cricket less attractive and interesting. But the habitues of Wantage Road became relatively early converts to the new format, thanks largely to this fixture against Warwickshire – only the second of the 'longer' games to be played at Northampton, and a real gem.

Northamptonshire were on top at the start, with West Indian Winston Davis (brought into the side after his fellow overseas player, Dennis Lillee, went down with a chest infection) and Alan Walker reducing Warwickshire to 58 for four, but Asif Din began the recovery and Dermot Reeve completed it on the second day as the visitors topped 400; usually an unassailable position in three-day cricket, although this was, of course, a different ball game. Their domination continued in the field through Tony Merrick and Paul Smith, whose three wickets in six balls included the adhesive Rob Bailey, and Andy Lloyd duly enforced the follow-on with a handsome lead of 245 and two days to go.

Northamptonshire collectively pulled themselves together and made a much better fist of it second time around. No one managed a century but most of the top-order men contributed handy runs, and although the spectre of defeat loomed very large again as 242 for four became 268 for eight – just 23 runs ahead with only two wickets standing – a gutsy ninth-wicket stand of 89 between wicketkeeper David Ripley and Davis at least made it all look a bit more respectable. The Bears might even lose a wicket or two in knocking off the 119 needed to win.

Indeed they might. Faced with an awkward forty-five-minute session before lunch on the final day, Warwickshire went in at 38 for four; Andy Moles and Geoff Humpage out to the tireless Davis, Andy Lloyd and Alvin Kallicharran falling to Walker, who then removed Smith to make it 51 for five. Asif Din and Reeve, the two first-innings centurions, restored a semblance of order by adding 47, but now the off-spin of Richard Williams caused a fresh

breach in the walls. His victims included, crucially, Asif for 48, and when Norman Gifford joined Gordon Parsons, Warwickshire were still 14 runs short. The last pair scored seven before the old warrior edged Williams low to acting-skipper Wayne Larkins at slip. Gifford didn't want to go and stood his ground, but David Evans' raised finger sent him on his way.

Northamptonshire had won after following on for the first time since Charlie Pool and George Thompson undid Worcestershire in 1906. It was also, remarkably, only their sixth victory over Warwickshire at Northampton in fifty-five attempts. They are still, in 2002, awaiting the seventh.

Winston Davis.

Warwickshire won the toss and elected to bat

Umpires: DGL Evans & JW Holder

WARWICKSHIRE

TA Lloyd*	b Davis	10	c Bailey b Walker	2
AJ Moles	b Davis	7	lbw b Davis	9
Asif Din	c Ripley b Walker	131	c Walker b Williams	48
AI Kallicharran	lbw b Davis	0	lbw b Walker	0
GW Humpage+	lbw b Walker	3	c&b Davis	3
PA Smith	lbw b Davis	47	c Williams b Walker	5
DA Reeve	b Williams	103	c Fordham b Davis	12
GJ Parsons	c Ripley b Davis	18	not out	8
TA Merrick	b Davis	34	b Williams	1
ARK Pierson	not out	18	b Davis	1
N Gifford	b Williams	12	c Larkins b Williams	3
Extras	(b1 lb8 w9 nb14)	32	(b8 lb2 nb10)	20
TOTAL		415		112

FOW 1st: 12,41,41,58,147,254,289,366,399
FOW 2nd: 3,22,24,38,51,98,103,104,105

Bowling 1st: Davis 36-5-141-6 Capel 22-5-75-0 Walker 25-9-67-2 Cook 34-11-57-0
Brown 14-5-34-0 Wild 9-0-22-0 Williams 3.2-0-10-2

Bowling 2nd: Davis 19-3-44-4 Capel 1-0-6-0 Walker 14-1-40-3 Cook 1-0-3-0
Williams 6.4-3-9-3

NORTHAMPTONSHIRE

A Fordham	lbw b Merrick	6	lbw b Parsons	26
W Larkins*	c Humpage b Parsons	19	c Humpage b Reeve	33
RJ Bailey	lbw b Smith	76	c Lloyd b Gifford	60
DJ Capel	c Reeve b Gifford	9	c Moles b Smith	37
RG Williams	c Humpage b Pierson	8	c Humpage b Merrick	13
DJ Wild	b Merrick	17	c&b Smith	58
D Ripley+	not out	14	c Lloyd b Reeve	47
NGB Cook	lbw b Smith	0	lbw b Merrick	1
SJE Brown	b Smith	0	c Humpage b Merrick	0
WW Davis	c Asif Din b Gifford	6	c Gifford b Smith	43
A Walker	c Moles b Merrick	0	not out	3
Extras	(b2 lb5 nb8)	15	(b5 lb10 w5 nb22)	42
TOTAL		170		363

FOW 1st: 11,49,78,105,132,149,149,151,163
FOW 2nd: 58,92,170,184,242,264,268,268,357

Bowling 1st: Merrick 19.5-3-48-3 Parsons 9-2-26-1 Gifford 18-7-38-2 Reeve 6-1-
16-0 Pierson 12-3-27-1 Smith 6-0-8-3

Bowling 2nd: Merrick 39-7-115-3 Parsons 17-5-36-1 Gifford 28-11-68-1 Reeve
18.3-6-30-2 Pierson 19-8-39-0 Smith 18-1-49-3 Asif Din 8-3-11-0

NORTHAMPTONSHIRE WON BY 6 RUNS

HAMPSHIRE

15 August 1990 at Southampton

Like Jim Griffiths before him, Mark Robinson's considerable merits as a bowler were less well known to many casual followers of the game than his shortcomings with the bat. In 1990, Robinson set a new record by failing to score in twelve successive first-class innings; but the same season also saw him usher Northamptonshire into the final of the NatWest Trophy with two outstanding efforts that marked him out as a cricketer with 'bottle'.

At the quarter-final stage, against Worcestershire at Northampton, he kept his head as the visitors closed in on their target of 264, and bowled both Neal Radford and Phil Newport at the end to help his side home by four runs. Then, at Southampton a fortnight later, he was called upon to send down the last over with Hampshire needing five to tie – possibly enough – and six to win, after Rajesh Maru had plundered two boundaries in the penultimate over from Curtly Ambrose. Robinson conceded only three from the first five balls, also dismissing Maru, and Paul-Jan Bakker failed to beat Allan Lamb's underarm return as he attempted the second run that would have taken Hampshire to Lord's. On both occasions the Man of the Match award went to a player on the losing team, but it was 'Robbo' – rather than Ian Botham or Malcolm Marshall – who would be playing at headquarters on the first Saturday in September.

It had been another fascinating semi, with the initiative shifting backwards and forwards throughout the day. Northamptonshire scored freely after being put in by Mark Nicholas, notably through Lamb and David Capel who added 66 in 11 overs, and then Richard Williams with 44 from 37 balls. Robinson struck an early blow as Hampshire began their reply, having Chris Smith held at backward point, but from 55 for three they rallied strongly through Marshall and David Gower. Both men survived chances as the county's fielding faltered, and their stand of 141 in 26 overs seemed likely to prove decisive.

At 196 for three, Hampshire still required 89 from 17 overs. Gower had been dropped by Curtly Ambrose at long-on just after completing his half-century, but he offered Northamptonshire another opportunity on 86 and this time Capel, in the same position, took

it. The fielder's aggressive reaction, picked up by the television cameras, earned him an official reprimand from the club, but Lamb's men were back in the game. Marshall and Nicholas piled on another 50 at eight-an-over until Nick Cook removed them both, and as the light faded – a rain-delayed start meant an 8.30 p.m. finish – Northamptonshire held their nerve to win.

Robinson again bowled tidily in the final, but by the time he had the ball in his hand, the match was effectively over; Northamptonshire rolled out for 171 by Lancashire, who won by seven wickets with more than 14 overs to spare. It was also, to the disappointment of many at Wantage Road, his last big game for the county. At the end of the season, the immensely likeable Hull-born seamer opted to join his native Yorkshire, later moving on to Sussex. Needless to say, his wickets were missed more than his runs.

Mark Robinson earns the congratulations of his team-mates after the pulsating final over at Southampton.

Hampshire won the toss and elected to field

Umpires: KJ Lyons & AGT Whitehead

NORTHAMPTONSHIRE

A Fordham	c Ayling b Bakker	1
NA Felton	c Gower b Connor	31
W Larkins	c Parks b Ayling	48
AJ Lamb*	c CL Smith b Maru	58
DJ Capel	c Nicholas b Maru	43
RJ Bailey	c Parks b Connor	8
RG Williams	b Connor	44
D Ripley+	c Maru b Marshall	7
CEL Ambrose	st Parks b Ayling	22
NGB Cook	not out	6
MA Robinson	b Connor	0
Extras	(lb6 w9 nb1)	16
TOTAL		284

FOW: 6,70,111,177,205,205,230,272,284

Bowling: Marshall 12-3-37-1 Bakker 12-2-41-1 Connor 12-1-73-4 Ayling 12-0-76-2 Maru 12-0-51-2

HAMPSHIRE

VP Terry	c Robinson b Cook	24
CL Smith	c Felton b Robinson	0
RA Smith	c Ripley b Capel	20
DI Gower	c Capel b Williams	86
MD Marshall	c&b Cook	77
MCJ Nicholas*	c Lamb b Cook	29
JR Ayling	c Williams b Robinson	8
RJ Parks+	c Felton b Ambrose	4
RJ Maru	c Capel b Robinson	10
CA Connor	not out	7
PJ Bakker	run out	2
Extras	(lb12 w4)	

FOW: 6,37,55,196,246,253,259,269,280

Bowling: Ambrose 12-4-29-1 Robinson 12-1-62-3 Cook 12-3-52-3 Capel 12-1-67-1 Williams 12-1-61-1

NORTHAMPTONSHIRE WON BY 1 RUN

LEICESTERSHIRE
5 September 1992 at Lord's

Aside from a few intriguing off-the-field subplots, the 1992 NatWest Trophy final threw up little to enthuse the neutral. It was a one-sided affair, all over by 6.15 p.m., with no centuries, no five-wicket (or even four-wicket) hauls and not even enough sunshine to get a tan. But Northamptonshire supporters couldn't have cared less. Beating Leicestershire is always satisfying; beating them in a Lord's final even better.

But who would be playing? On the one hand, all-rounder Vince Wells was taken ill and Leicestershire considered calling up one of their 'old boys', Jonathan Agnew or Peter Willey, before deciding to take a risk on the half-fit David Millns. On the other, Curtly Ambrose – Northamptonshire's key bowler, whose spell of four for seven in 8.3 overs killed off Yorkshire's challenge in the second round – failed to appear at the team's hotel the night before, and frantic messages passed for a time between Swiss Cottage and St John's Wood, where chief executive Steve Coverdale was attending the Cricket Writers' Club dinner, as the search for Curtly gathered momentum. He eventually pitched up at nine o'clock, and Coverdale could at least enjoy his pudding and cheese in peace, secure in the knowledge that the big man hadn't been kidnapped.

There was also the ongoing saga of Allan Lamb and the alleged ball-tamperers. The county skipper's revelations in the *Daily Mirror* earned him fines from his own club and the T.C.C.B., not to mention the threat of legal action from his old team-mate, Sarfraz Nawaz. There was even talk of a writ being served on him as he walked out to bat in the final. This was much more interesting for the tabloids than the outcome of a private cricketing quarrel between two old East Midlands rivals which hadn't even managed to fill the ground.

Having disposed of Warwickshire in a low-scoring, attritional semi-final at Edgbaston, Northamptonshire took an early grip at Lord's with Leicestershire's openers, Tim Boon and Nigel Briers, run out by Kevin Curran and Rob Bailey respectively. James Whitaker and Phil Robinson dug in to add 130, and it wasn't until the fifty-fourth over that a wicket fell to a bowler – Whitaker caught off Curran for 84. Five men then departed for 25 in the space of 33 balls, and Leicestershire's final total was a modest one.

The tremors caused by Nigel Felton's early dismissal soon abated as Alan Fordham and Bailey took charge, although it might have been different had Justin Benson – bowled for a duck by Curtly Ambrose earlier in the day – not dropped both men in the slips. Fordham, who hit 13 fours in his 140-ball innings, went just before the end, and it was left to Bailey to score the winning runs off the luckless Benson with more than ten overs to spare. The victorious skipper was soon brandishing Northamptonshire's third one-day trophy, looking down from the pavilion balcony at the 'Wham-Bam Allan Lamb' banners in the crowd below. Lamb's England career may have been over, but his beloved 'wheel of fortune' still had an interesting revolution or two in store.

Drawing-room champagne for the 1992 NatWest Trophy winners.

Northamptonshire won the toss and elected to field ·

Umpires: DJ Constant & DR Shepherd

LEICESTERSHIRE

TJ Boon	run out	3
NE Briers*	run out	25
JJ Whitaker	c Taylor b Curran	84
PE Robinson	c Felton b Ambrose	62
JDR Benson	b Ambrose	0
L Potter	c Capel b Curran	12
WKM Benjamin	b Curran	0
PA Nixon+	not out	7
GJ Parsons	not out	1
AD Mullally		
DJ Millns		
Extras	(b1 lb8 w3 nb2)	14
TOTAL	(7 wkts)	208

FOW: 3,45,175,178,197,198,200

Bowling: Ambrose 12-0-35-2 Taylor 7-1-19-0 Capel 11-3-39-0 Curran 12-1-41-3
Cook 12-0-43-0 Penberthy 6-0-22-0

NORTHAMPTONSHIRE

A Fordham	c Potter b Mullally	91
NA Felton	b Mullally	6
RJ Bailey	not out	72
AJ Lamb*	not out	24
DJ Capel		
KM Curran		
AL Penberthy		
D Ripley+		
CEL Ambrose		
JP Taylor		
NGB Cook		
Extras	(lb9 w9)	18
TOTAL	(2 wkts)	211

FOW: 29,173

Bowling: Benjamin 12-0-65-0 Mullally 10-2-22-0 Millns 10-0-43-0 Parsons 9-1-31-0 Potter 4-0-18-0 Benson 4.4-1-23-0

NORTHAMPTONSHIRE WON BY 8 WICKETS

WARWICKSHIRE

27, 28, 29, 31 July 1995 at Edgbaston

The 'beamers-and-barneys' rivalry between Northamptonshire and Warwickshire in the 1990s was intense and occasionally bitter. That being so, it came as something of a surprise to find their respective captains in total agreement, but Allan Lamb and Dermot Reeve both described this titanic struggle in Birmingham as the best County Championship match they had ever played in. It was four-day cricket at its very best, albeit a draining experience for players and spectators alike.

Northamptonshire went into the game trailing their neighbours – the defending champions and favourites to retain the title – by 17 points, and when Allan Donald and Tim Munton dismissed Lamb's team by mid-afternoon on the opening day, it seemed unlikely that the county would be able to narrow that gap. The only serious resistance came from Northamptonshire's supreme competitor, David Capel, whose half-century included a top-edged six off Donald. Cruising at 67 without loss in reply, Warwickshire then fell foul of a fired-up Capel – three wickets in four overs – and they were indebted to Roger Twose, who reached 98 overnight and was eventually last out for 140, Capel's seventh victim of the innings, after five-and-a-half hours at the crease. Thanks to Twose's patience and tenacity, Warwickshire led by 72. Northamptonshire lost Richard Montgomerie, Rob Bailey and Mal Loye in clearing the arrears, but Alan Fordham survived an early chance and set about emulating Twose. He reached his hundred in five hours just before the close, and at 254 for six the visitors were 182 in front with two days to go; this despite another heroic effort from Donald, who picked up three wickets in a 13-over spell after tea on one of the hottest, stickiest days of the year.

Donald removed Fordham first thing next morning, but Russell Warren strengthened Northamptonshire's advantage – their last four wickets adding 144 – and Warwickshire needed 275 to win. John Hughes dismissed Wasim Khan at 14; then Anil Kumble, the brisk leg-spinner from Bangalore who was proving an inspired overseas signing, snapped up four for 32 in 16 overs, and the home side were 53 for six just after tea. Enter Neil Smith to join his captain, and the seventh-wicket pair transformed the match again with a stand of 148 that lasted into the final day. They carried Warwickshire to within 74 of their target until Kumble broke through again; it was Northamptonshire's match after all, at 228 for nine. But Donald and Munton were not about to bow to the seemingly inevitable and put on 39 before 'Fiery' Capel trapped the latter in front.

All were given a standing ovation as they left the field. 'It was a bit of a war out there,' admitted Lamb afterwards. 'No one budged an inch – and that's the way it should be.' And Warwickshire ended the season by far the happier of the two teams, as winners of both the Championship and the NatWest Trophy. In the 60-over decider at Lord's, they beat Northamptonshire by four wickets, proving the old adage that the only victory that really matters is the final one.

Northamptonshire's players leave the field in triumph after completing their narrow victory.

Northamptonshire won the toss and elected to bat

Umpires: R Julian & KE Palmer

NORTHAMPTONSHIRE

RR Montgomerie	b Donald	6		c Ostler b Munton	29
A Fordham	b Donald	8		c Piper b Donald	101
RJ Bailey	lbw b Munton	7		c Piper b Brown	2
MB Loye	c Smith b Munton	12		c Piper b Munton	6
AJ Lamb*	c Piper b Reeve	22		b Donald	22
KM Curran	b Brown	10		c Brown b Donald	30
DJ Capel	c Ostler b Munton	50		c Singh b Donald	17
RJ Warren+	c Ostler b Donald	20		c Reeve b Donald	70
A Kumble	c Piper b Donald	0		c Ostler b Brown	21
JG Hughes	c Reeve b Munton	0	(11)	not out	4
JP Taylor	not out	4	(10)	c Piper b Donald	3
Extras	(b4 lb3 nb6)	13		(b9 lb11 w1 nb20)	41
TOTAL		152			346

FOW 1st: 14,23,23,45,69,69,120,120,125
FOW 2nd: 57,60,71,124,182,202,278,337,339

Bowling 1st: Donald 16-8-41-4 Munton 20.3-6-47-4 Reeve 12-4-26-1 Brown 7-0-31-1

Bowling 2nd: Donald 39.1-10-95-6 Munton 29-8-83-2 Reeve 6-1-25-0 Brown 23-9-51-2 Smith 21-4-72-0

WARWICKSHIRE

RG Twose	c Kumble b Capel	140	b Capel	16
WG Khan	b Capel	17	lbw b Hughes	3
DP Ostler	lbw b Capel	0	c Lamb b Kumble	14
TL Penney	c Curran b Capel	1	c Bailey b Kumble	0
A Singh	b Kumble	5	c Montgomerie b Kumble	7
DR Brown	b Kumble	0	c Warren b Kumble	4
DA Reeve*	c Bailey b Capel	14	c Bailey b Kumble	74
NMK Smith	b Capel	18	b Kumble	75
KJ Piper+	c Curran b Capel	0	c&b Kumble	10
AA Donald	c Montgomerie b Kumble	9	not out	27
TA Munton	not out	0	lbw b Capel	10
Extras	(lb12 nb8)	20	(b8 lb11 nb8)	27
TOTAL		224		267

FOW 1st: 67,67,79,108,108,145,181,181,218
FOW 2nd: 14,32,37,42,52,53,201,225,228

Bowling 1st: Taylor 17-3-41-0 Curran 7-0-26-0 Kumble 29-7-69-3 Hughes 7-2-32-0 Capel 18.5-3-44-7

Bowling 2nd: Taylor 31-6-78-0 Curran 5-1-17-0 Kumble 42-16-82-7 Hughes 12-3-29-1 Capel 19-9-26-2 Bailey 4-1-16-0

NORTHAMPTONSHIRE WON BY 7 RUNS

NOTTINGHAMSHIRE

24, 25, 26, 28 August 1995 at Northampton

Dennis Brookes made 492 first-class appearances for Northamptonshire between 1934 and 1959, and in 2001 – the year of his eighty-sixth birthday – was still an avid follower of the county's fortunes at Wantage Road. So when he declared after the Championship match against Nottinghamshire in late-August 1995 that he had 'never seen anything like it,' cricket aficionados took notice.

It was a year replete with extraordinary games. Thirty wickets fell on the first day when Essex visited Luton, and Northamptonshire still managed to win after being dismissed for 46. They were skittled out for 59 by Surrey at Northampton, and won that one too. Not to mention the epic at Edgbaston, which has already been described. But there were moments during the contest with Nottinghamshire when you half-expected to see Graham Chapman's army officer from *Monty Python's Flying Circus* appear on the field and complain that it was all 'getting silly'.

From Northamptonshire's point of view, the opening day was more tragic than comic. Still in contention for a first Championship title, they managed only one wicket – Paul Pollard falling to Anil Kumble's sixth ball of the match. Tim Robinson, dropped at second slip off Kevin Curran with three to his name, was still there at the close on 204, with Nottinghamshire 353 for one. His second-wicket stand with Graeme Archer was worth 294, and although the rest of the batting fell away, the visitors were still in a powerful position when Northamptonshire began their reply, needing 378 to avoid the follow-on.

But runs flowed rapidly right from the start. Openers Alan Fordham and Richard Montgomerie put 149 on the board in the last 44 overs of Friday's play, and the county scored another 560 on Saturday for the loss of seven wickets. There were three centuries; from

Anil Kumble bowls to Nottinghamshire's last man, Andy Afford – victory is only moments away.

Fordham, Allan Lamb – who, on 70, became only the fifth batsman to notch 20,000 first-class runs for Northamptonshire – and a maiden effort from Russell Warren. With the weather set fair, Lamb opted to go for a big lead and let Kumble loose again. To that end, he kept Nottinghamshire in the field for another 51 balls on Monday morning and 72 more runs were added, David Capel becoming the fourth centurion.

The visitors went in again facing a deficit of 254, and at 72 for one it was odds-on a draw. Then Robinson, Paul Johnson and Archer went in the space of eight deliveries, and Kumble worked his way down the order with the aid of some excellent close catching. Wayne Noon, nursing a bruised jaw, held up his former county for 47 overs, and when he was dropped in the gully off Paul Taylor – Kumble and Tony Penberthy colliding – it looked as though Nottinghamshire might still get away with it. But the next ball, from a slightly dizzy Kumble, had Andy Afford leg-before, and Northamptonshire were there with 2.5 overs to spare. The statisticians scurried off to re-write their record books – no team had ever registered over 500 and lost by an innings – and everyone else pinched themselves to make sure they hadn't dreamt it all.

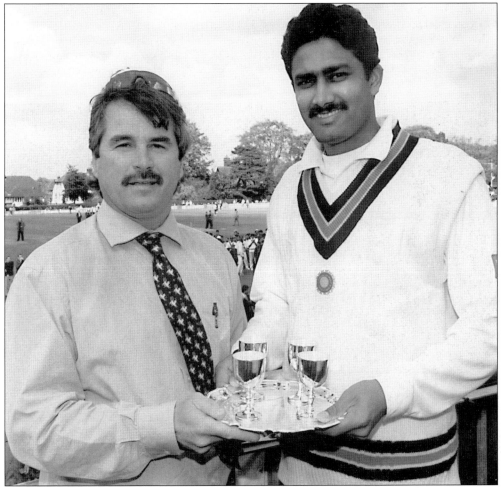

Two key figures in Northamptonshire's eventful 1995 season – skipper Allan Lamb and Anil Kumble.

David Capel takes the applause after becoming Northamptonshire's fourth centurion of the innings.

Nottinghamshire won the toss and elected to bat

Umpires: JH Harris & NT Plews

NOTTINGHAMSHIRE

PR Pollard	c Capel b Kumble	30		b Curran	16
RT Robinson*	lbw b Curran	209		b Kumble	31
GF Archer	lbw b Capel	158		lbw b Capel	17
P Johnson	c Lamb b Curran	4		c&b Kumble	0
CL Cairns	c Lamb b Taylor	0	(6)	c Montgomerie b Kumble	11
MP Dowman	c Capel b Kumble	8	(5)	c Snape b Curran	2
WM Noon+	c Montgomerie b Kumble	33	(8)	not out	25
JE Hindson	lbw b Capel	9	(7)	c Warren b Curran	4
RA Pick	lbw b Kumble	11		c Montgomerie b Kumble	23
RJ Chapman	not out	11		c Fordham b Taylor	5
JA Afford	lbw b Curran	12		lbw b Kumble	0
Extras	(b9 lb15 nb18)	42		(b6 lb8 w1 nb8)	23
TOTAL		527			157

FOW 1st: 68,362,372,373,419,457,475,487,502
FOW 2nd: 24,72,72,72,85,85,90,133,150

Bowling 1st: Taylor 27-8-59-1 Curran 29.1-5-97-3 Capel 23-1-84-2 Penberthy 14-1-59-0 Kumble 50-15-118-4 Snape 14-2-59-0 Bailey 8-0-27-0

Bowling 2nd: Taylor 15-3-40-1 Curran 19-7-39-3 Capel 8-3-16-1 Kumble 39.1-21-43-5 Snape 4-3-1-0 Bailey 3-2-4-0

NORTHAMPTONSHIRE

RR Montgomerie	c Pollard b Cairns	69
A Fordham	c Noon b Pick	130
RJ Bailey	c Pollard b Afford	3
AJ Lamb*	c Johnson b Hindson	115
RJ Warren	lbw b Afford	154
KM Curran	c Noon b Afford	70
DJ Capel	not out	114
AL Penberthy	c Robinson b Hindson	35
JN Snape	not out	27
A Kumble		
JP Taylor		
Extras	(b9 lb21 w10 nb24)	64
TOTAL	(7 wkts dec)	781

FOW 1st: 188,205,253,412,567,609,709

Bowling 1st: Cairns 26-4-65-1 Pick 24-3-119-1 Chapman 21-1-109-0 Hindson 33-4-160-2 Afford 41-4-223-3 Archer 12-3-45-0 Dowman 5-0-30-0

NORTHAMPTONSHIRE WON BY AN INNINGS AND 97 RUNS

WARWICKSHIRE

11, 12 June 1996 at Northampton

For Northamptonshire, 1996 was Year One A.L. – After Lamb. He had already handed over the captaincy at the end of the previous season, and in March announced his retirement from the first-class game to avoid T.C.C.B. censorship of his forthcoming autobiography. The new leadership team of Rob Bailey – as skipper – and player-coach John Emburey took the team into the semi-finals of the Benson & Hedges Cup where Warwickshire awaited them. The talk, inevitably, was of exacting revenge for defeat in the NatWest final of 1995.

In the thirty-first over, with Northamptonshire sagging at 88 for six after being put in by Dermot Reeve, it appeared to be a case of 'roll on 1997'. Of the top-order batsmen, only Richard Montgomerie made any impression with a solid 49 from 76 balls. It was down to Tim Walton, the twenty-three-year-old Yorkshireman preferred to Alan Fordham just before the start, and Cornishman Tony Penberthy to try and give the bowlers something to defend, and they responded by adding 108 in 17 overs – a Northamptonshire seventh-wicket record in all one-day competitions.

Walton's first-class opportunities had been severely limited since he joined the staff in 1991, but with his natural flamboyance – even down to the raffish bandanna worn under the helmet – he was a natural for one-day cricket; a hard-hitting batsman who could also send down a few overs of medium pace, and a brilliant fielder. Just how brilliant, Warwickshire would soon discover. For now, he and Penberthy revived the county's flagging hopes of a return to Lord's, Walton's unbeaten 70 coming off 73 deliveries with 2 sixes and 5 fours. The visitors had reached 91 for three in the twenty-fourth over when rain stopped play and forced the match into a second day. It was, at that stage, too close to call.

Next morning, Dominic Ostler and Paul Smith moved the total on to 118 before Curtly Ambrose got through Ostler with a rapid yorker. Smith found another reliable partner in Trevor Penney, who at 146 swung one down to deep mid-wicket where Walton was on patrol. Penney,

himself one of the deadliest fielders in the game, turned for the second run – only to see Walton's superb skimming return hit the stumps on the first bounce. In the next over, Smith pushed Paul Taylor to backward point and set off for a single; the same thrower, the same result – this time at the bowler's end – and Warwickshire struggling at 151 for six. When Shaun Pollock skied David Capel to long-on six runs later, the issue was all but settled.

Walton was a straightforward choice as Man of the Match, and shone briefly in the final with 28 from 26 balls as Northamptonshire went down to defeat at Lancashire's hands by 31 runs. But his glory was sadly short-lived; released by the club a couple of years later, he was out of the county game altogether by the end of 1999. What a waste.

Tim Walton – this was his finest hour ...

Warwickshire won the toss and elected to field

Umpires: JC Balderstone & JH Hampshire

NORTHAMPTONSHIRE

DJ Capel	c Piper b Brown	7
RR Montgomerie	c Giles b PA Smith	49
RJ Bailey*	b Welch	10
MB Loye	run out	1
KM Curran	b Reeve	3
RJ Warren+	c Piper b PA Smith	10
TC Walton	not out	70
AL Penberthy	c Brown b Pollock	41
JE Emburey	not out	2
CEL Ambrose		
JP Taylor		
Extras	(lb8 w11 nb8)	
TOTAL	(7 wkts)	220

FOW: 15,42,58,69,83,88,196

Bowling: Pollock 10-2-41-1 Brown 10-1-46-1 Welch 10-1-32-1 Reeve 10-2-30-1 PA Smith 9-0-56-2 NMK Smith 1-0-7-0

WARWICKSHIRE

AJ Moles	c Penberthy b Curran	33
NMK Smith	c Ambrose b Taylor	15
DR Brown	b Taylor	0
DP Ostler	b Ambrose	33
PA Smith	run out	45
TL Penney	run out	14
SM Pollock	c Loye b Capel	7
DA Reeve*	not out	21
G Welch	lbw b Emburey	1
KJ Piper+	run out	7
AF Giles	run out	8
Extras	(lb7 w2)	9
TOTAL		193

FOW: 34,36,61,118,147,151,157,159,172

Bowling: Ambrose 9-0-39-1 Taylor 10-1-25-2 Capel 10-0-29-1 Curran 6-0-32-1 Penberthy 4-0-30-0 Emburey 8.5-1-31-1

NORTHAMPTONSHIRE WON BY 27 RUNS

GLAMORGAN

21, 22, 23, 24 May 1998 at Northampton

Malachy Loye, Northampton-born of Irish parents, played much of his early cricket in Cogenhoe, once the home village of the great George Thompson. In the latter's heyday, 10 hours 48 minutes of playing time was regularly sufficient to complete an entire match; in 1998, the former spent that long at the crease to create new Northamptonshire records for both the longest and highest individual innings in first-class cricket.

It was a staggering performance, born of adversity. Northamptonshire never fully recovered after crashing to 45 for five on the first morning, and by the close the reigning county champions were already 32 runs ahead with eight wickets standing. Steve James eventually perished one run short of Roy Fredericks' record score for Glamorgan against the county, hitting 36 fours in a stay of six-and-a-quarter hours and adding 186 in 38 overs with Michael Powell. Tony Cottey heaped on more misery to become the third century-maker, and Northamptonshire were batting again on the second evening, needing 391 to avoid losing by an innings.

Loye, an enigmatic player capable of brilliance but desperately unlucky with injuries in his first few seasons at Wantage Road, came to the crease at 5 for one early on Saturday, and got off the mark first ball by pulling Waqar Younis to the boundary. While he settled to his task, wickets fell at the other end; the demise of Kevin Curran brought in David Ripley at 142 for four, and it seemed impossible that Northamptonshire would be getting out of this one. But Loye and Ripley thought otherwise and were still together at the close, their partnership already worth 269 and Loye unbeaten on 201.

Sunday saw 40,000 Northampton Town fans head to Wembley for the Division Two play-off final against Grimsby Town, and only the county die-hards were in attendance to see the pair resume their rearguard action. The stand had reached 401 – a fifth-wicket record in English first-class cricket – when Ripley fell to Cottey's off-spin, but Loye pressed remorselessly on. Just after three o'clock, he cut Steve Watkin to the fence at backward point and passed Raman Subba Row's 300 against Surrey in 1958. The game was now safe, and he carried his tally of boundaries to 49 before running out of partners at 712 – the highest second-innings total in Championship history. Glamorgan played out time while the records section of *Wisden* was pored over by everyone in the ground.

Among the congratulatory faxes was one from Subba Row, warning Loye to watch out for a new record-breaker in forty years' time. For the moment, it was a hugely satisfying 'Local Boy Makes Good' story, and Loye realised just how delighted his fellow Northamptonians were when he went out for a meal that Sunday evening. The restaurateur, a keen county supporter, declined to present a bill.

Northamptonshire's first two triple-centurions, Mal Loye (right) and Raman Subba Row, 1998.

Glamorgan won the toss and elected to field

Umpires: NG Cowley & B Leadbeater

NORTHAMPTONSHIRE

RR Montgomerie	c Shaw b Watkin	1		lbw b Watkin	2
AJ Swann	c Powell b Waqar	5		lbw b Waqar	2
MB Loye	lbw b Thomas	29		not out	322
RJ Bailey	c Cosker b Waqar	4	(10)	c Shaw b Dale	32
DJG Sales	c Evans b Thomas	0	(4)	c Evans b Watkin	22
KM Curran*	c James b Dale	54	(5)	lbw b Waqar	21
D Ripley+	b Watkin	59	(6)	c Waqar b Cottey	209
GP Swann	lbw b Butcher	4	(7)	c Cosker b Thomas	17
JP Taylor	b Watkin	0	(8)	c James b Waqar	0
FA Rose	not out	3	(9)	c&b Thomas	10
DE Malcolm	b Butcher	2		c Dale b Thomas	42
Extras	(lb5 w4 nb2)	11		(b12 lb5 w6 nb10)	33
TOTAL		172			712

FOW 1st: 1,9,21,29,45,135,165,165,169
FOW 2nd: 5,15,72,142,543,562,565,584,663

Bowling 1st: Waqar 12-1-54-2 Watkin 15-5-30-3 Thomas 7-0-27-2 Butcher 7.2-2-22-2 Dale 9-2-25-1 Cosker 1-0-9-0

Bowling 2nd: Waqar 35-2-147-3 Watkin 34-5-131-2 Thomas 31.5-3-154-3 Butcher 17-1-79-0 Cosker 39-12-107-0 Dale 11-0-63-1 Cottey 6-2-14-1

GLAMORGAN

SP James	c Ripley b GP Swann	227	not out	10
AW Evans	b Malcolm	10	not out	25
A Dale	b Malcolm	45		
MJ Powell	c GP Swann b Sales	106		
PA Cottey*	c Curran b Taylor	113		
GP Butcher	c Ripley b Rose	1		
AD Shaw+	c AJ Swann b Malcolm	0		
Waqar Younis	c Taylor b Rose	2		
SD Thomas	b Taylor	17		
DA Cosker	c Ripley b Taylor	3		
SL Watkin	not out	1		
Extras	(b6 lb16 w2 nb14)	38	(b4 lb1 nb4)	9
TOTAL		563	(0 wkt)	44

FOW 1st: 25,169,355,447,454,469,478,524,544

FOW 2nd: -

Bowling 1st: Malcolm 28-3-144-3 Rose 28-3-130-2 Taylor 25.5-1-105-3 Curran 5-3-24-0 GP Swann 24-3-98-1 Bailey 1-1-0-0 Sales 9-2-28-1 AJ Swann 3-0-12-0

Bowling 2nd: Rose 4-1-15-0 Taylor 2-0-20-0 AJ Swann 1-0-4-0

MATCH DRAWN

GLOUCESTERSHIRE

30, 31 August, 1, 2 September 2000 at Northampton

Not since the end of 1904 had Northamptonshire been designated a 'second-class county,' but they effectively regained that appellation in 2000, courtesy of the E.C.B.'s decision – made for a variety of stated reasons, some of them apparently contradictory – to institute a two-division County Championship. Finishing thirteenth in 1999, the last summer of the old-style competition, condemned the county to Division Two. Director of cricket Bob Carter, in the second season of his third spell with the club, and captain Matthew Hayden, were only too well aware of the importance of escaping from it at the earliest possible opportunity.

To do so, Northamptonshire needed to claim one of the top three places. After a poor start to the campaign, which left them bottom of the table after losing to Glamorgan at Northampton on 9 July, the promotion challenge began to gather momentum. Warwickshire and Worcestershire were beaten; then Sussex twice, home and away; and Gloucestershire arrived at Wantage Road at the end of August looking to prevent Hayden's team from making it five Championship victories on the trot.

With the two off-spinners, Jason Brown and Graeme Swann, regarded as Northamptonshire's trump cards, Carter and Hayden had been putting their faith in a simple game plan – post a substantial total, even if that meant forgoing batting bonus points, and allow the bowlers to build pressure with a weight of runs behind them. In this instance, Tony Penberthy's first Championship century for more than a year was the most substantial contribution as Northamptonshire extended their innings well into the second day. Despite the absence of the younger Swann through injury – brother Alec took his place – Plan A was working to perfection again. Gloucestershire struggled against Brown and the pace of Darren Cousins, who was enjoying a new lease of life after joining the club from Essex, and followed on 283 behind just after five o'clock on the third evening.

Given good weather, Hayden was confident of finishing the job on Saturday. But, to his frus-

tration, there was rain about, and Gloucestershire's task was made easier by three stoppages which ate into the day's ration of overs and time. Northamptonshire were still on top at 110 for five, only for skipper Mark Alleyne and the apparently immovable Jack Russell to dig in and add 59 in 30 overs for the sixth wicket. Hayden had to try something different, and called up his former England left-arm paceman Paul Taylor to experiment with a spot of left-arm spin. The move paid off handsomely; Taylor accounted for both Alleyne and Russell, leaving Cousins to mop up the tail with a burst of three wickets in nine balls. Victory, with ten deliveries to spare, made that hoped-for promotion all but certain.

Tony Penberthy.

Northamptonshire won the toss and elected to bat

Umpires: GI Burgess & P Willey

NORTHAMPTONSHIRE

AS Rollins	lbw b Lewis	49
ML Hayden*	c Russell b Ball	41
JW Cook	b Cotterell	4
DJG Sales	b Ball	55
RJ Warren	c Snape b Lewis	61
AL Penberthy	b Snape	116
JP Taylor	b Alleyne	20
AJ Swann	not out	61
D Ripley+	c Russell b Snape	10
DM Cousins	b Snape	15
JF Brown	c Hewson b Ball	2
Extras	(b14 lb13 w2 nb6)	35
TOTAL		469

FOW 1st: 82,91,123,185,280,314,420,442,464

Bowling 1st: Lewis 32-11-96-2 Alleyne 26-12-51-1 Hancock 8-2-15-0 Ball 53-14-120-3 Cotterell 33-8-90-1 Snape 27-4-70-3

GLOUCESTERSHIRE

THC Hancock	lbw b Brown	22	c Ripley b Brown		9
DR Hewson	c Hayden b Brown	45	c&b Swann		39
MGN Windows	lbw b Brown	2	c Cook b Brown		36
KJ Barnett	lbw b Cousins	5	c Rollins b Swann		13
MCJ Ball	b Taylor	15 (9)	c Sales b Cousins		12
MW Alleyne*	lbw b Cousins	4 (5)	c Hayden b Taylor		18
CG Taylor	c Rollins b Brown	8 (6)	b Brown		6
RC Russell+	c Ripley b Cousins	40 (7)	b Taylor		41
JN Snape	c Hayden b Swann	15 (8)	not out		23
J Lewis	c Rollins b Cousins	22	c Ripley b Cousins		0
TP Cotterell	not out	0	c Sales b Cousins		0
Extras	(lb6 nb2)	8	(b7 lb5)		12
TOTAL		186			209

FOW 1st: 44,60,65,75,84,97,119,151,183
FOW 2nd: 21,60,104,104,110,169,176,202,207

Bowling 1st: Cousins 20-10-41-4 Taylor 20-4-59-1 Brown 34-12-68-4 Swann 6-2-12-1

Bowling 2nd: Cousins 24.2-9-38-3 Taylor 20-6-45-2 Brown 43-17-84-3 Swann 22-11-30-2

NORTHAMPTONSHIRE WON BY AN INNINGS AND 74 RUNS

ESSEX
27, 28, 29, 30 July 2001 at Northampton

For double-decker buses, read triple-centuries for Northamptonshire – nothing for ages, then three come along at once. A little over a year after Mal Loye's unbeaten 322 against Glamorgan, David Sales hit 303 not out against Essex and might have eclipsed Loye's score had last man Michael Davies not been run out after adding 88 with his senior partner. Then, in 2001, the same county's bowlers felt the weight of Mike Hussey's bat.

The twenty-six-year-old left-hander from Western Australia, signed to replace Matthew Hayden, took a while to come to terms with conditions in a damp English spring. However, he was averaging 50 in Championship cricket when Ronnie Irani's team – struggling, like Northamptonshire, at the wrong end of the Division One table – arrived at Wantage Road. David Ripley won an important toss and took first use of yet another batsman-friendly Northampton pitch, allowing Hussey to set out his stall for a long stay. He was still there on 200 at the close, with the county 378 for three, and passed milestone after milestone next day. A single off Peter Such shortly after lunch made him only the sixth Australian to reach 300 in England, and another push for one off Tim Phillips relegated Loye's knock to second place in Northamptonshire's all-time list.

Hussey hit a six and 48 fours in his ten-and-a-quarter hours at the crease, and received excellent support from Adrian Rollins, Loye himself and Tony Penberthy, all of whom shared in three-figure stands. In the course of his innings, Hussey also became the first player since Roger Prideaux in 1962 to pass 1,000 runs in his debut season for Northamptonshire. But now there was fielding to be done, and he spent the next two-and-a-bit days urging his team-mates on in pursuit of the side's elusive first Championship win of the summer.

Paul Grayson proved a formidable obstacle, batting for a total of ten-and-a-half hours, and at 283 for five in the final session of the match, Essex looked to have secured a draw. Then the spinners, Jason Brown and Graeme Swann, ran through the rest in double-quick time – the last four wickets falling for two runs in 28 balls – and Northamptonshire faced a run-chase; 95 to win in 15 overs. Hussey, who had been on the field throughout the match, seized the moment and smashed 70 not out from 33 deliveries, easing the county home with four overs to spare.

It was a triumph made possible by Hussey's technique, stamina, determination and self-confidence – but he remained suitably modest about it all, admitting that he found it 'a bit embarrassing' to join Trumper, Armstrong, Macartney, Bradman and Simpson in the ranks of his countryman to notch a triple-ton on English soil. Had anyone come across even a *slightly* embarrassed Australian cricketer before? His efforts couldn't save Northamptonshire from relegation in 2001, but his personal qualities were recognised with the award of the captaincy for the following season when returning to the top flight would be the club's overriding priority.

Northamptonshire won the toss and elected to bat

Umpires: MJ Harris & AGT Whitehead

NORTHAMPTONSHIRE

MEK Hussey	not out	329	not out	70
AS Rollins	b Such	39	not out	21
MB Loye	lbw b Irani	52		
RJ Warren	c Foster b Phillips	38		
AL Penberthy	c&b Grayson	101		
TMB Bailey	c Foster b Such	25		
GP Swann	b Such	1		
D Ripley*+	not out	19		
JP Taylor				
MR Strong				
JF Brown				
Extras	(b7 lb6 w8 nb8)	29	(lb1 w2 nb2)	5
TOTAL	(6 wkts dec)	633	(0 wkts)	96

FOW 1st: 135,237,320,530,588,606
FOW 2nd: -

Bowling 1st: Cowan 26-3-105-0 Irani 15-3-45-1 Such 53-13-182-3 Phillips 33-3-144-1 Napier 14-2-59-0 Grayson 21-2-85-1

Bowling 2nd: Irani 6-0-43-0 Cowan 4-0-36-0 Grayson 1-0-16-0

ESSEX

RS Clinton	lbw b Taylor	5	c Ripley b Strong	1
AP Grayson	c Hussey b Swann	173	lbw b Taylor	149
DDJ Robinson	c Ripley b Taylor	63	c Ripley b Brown	31
SG Law	c Ripley b Penberthy	12	b Strong	48
RC Irani*	c Hussey b Taylor	5	c Hussey b Brown	14
SD Peters	c Rollins b Swann	6	c Bailey b Brown	13
JS Foster+	c Ripley b Penberthy	79	c Rollins b Swann	16
GR Napier	c Ripley b Strong	35	b Swann	9
TJ Phillips	lbw b Swann	25	lbw b Brown	0
AP Cowan	not out	15	b Brown	1
PM Such	lbw b Penberthy	0	not out	0
Extras	(b4 lb4 nb4)	12	(b9 lb6)	15
TOTAL		430		297

FOW 1st: 11,208,245,253,260,279,347,411,419
FOW 2nd: 4,66,178,209,235,283,295,296,296

Bowling 1st: Strong 24-7-66-1 Taylor 28-4-85-3 Brown 32-5-101-0 Penberthy 16-2-60-3 Swann 32-10-96-3 Hussey 2-0-14-0

Bowling 2nd: Strong 13-3-57-2 Taylor 13-6-30-1 Penberthy 5-3-6-0 Brown 40.2-10-107-5 Swann 29-6-82-2

NORTHAMPTONSHIRE WON BY 10 WICKETS

More runs on the way for Mike Hussey.